# The Dinkum Dictionary

Susan Butler is publisher of *The Ma*          ...nd
has been a member of its editorial co...          ... 1980.
She writes a words column for the Melb...      *...ge*.

# The Dinkum Dictionary

## THE ORIGINS OF AUSTRALIAN WORDS

### SECOND EDITION

Susan Butler

TEXT PUBLISHING

MELBOURNE AUSTRALIA

ACKNOWLEDGMENTS
Special thanks to Maureen Leslie and Alison Moore for all their help in
reading and preparing word entries for this book.

The Text Publishing Company
171 La Trobe Street
Melbourne Victoria 3000
Australia

First published 2001, reprinted 2001
This edition 2003, reprinted 2003

Printed and bound by Griffin Press
Typeset in Janson 11/15 by J&M Typesetting

National Library of Australia
Cataloguing-in-Publication data:

Butler, Susan, 1948- .

The dinkum dictionary : the origins of Australian words.
2nd edition

ISBN 1 877008 48 6.

1. English language - Australia. 2. English language -
Australia - Dictionaries. I. Title.

427.994

# foreword

In this second edition of *The Dinkum Dictionary* I have selected over fifty new entries from various aspects of Australian life. Some of these words relate to our environment, such as 'mallee' and 'baobab', and some, such as 'Eureka stockade' and 'blind Freddy', are from our history and popular culture. Other words chosen draw heavily on the languages of Australia's Aboriginal peoples and include 'kurdaitcha man' and 'pialla'. Each is a dinkum addition to the set of words that defines us as Australian and that gives a unique stamp to our kind of English.

# our language, our past
# the origins of Australian words

Language is a constant stream in our society, a current that gives shape to our thoughts in all kinds of contexts. It can be bland, entertaining, cajoling, abusive, eloquent or stilted but it is ever present. If we slow down to look at this stream more closely we will find words that are like pebbles in the water—full of interest and discovery.

In following the origins of these words we can see the pathways to the present. We can see, in the words that we have taken to be our own, where we have borrowed, where we have been inventive and where we have adapted words to our own use. This is what makes each kind of English different and special—the fact that different communities have taken English and shaped it to fit their unique experience of the world, wherever that may be.

The easiest identifier of a variety of English is, of course, accent. We have no difficulty telling an American from a British speaker, an Australian from a South African, an Indian from a Singaporean. And our response to accent is often emotional. There's no place like home and, for us, there's no accent like an Australian one.

Our particular accent was forged by the children of the first convicts. Their parents may have arrived in the colony with every conceivable British dialect, but the children, with their desire to conform to each other, blended these dialectal features into one shared sound pattern. There have been some changes to the accent since then—mostly making it sound more like what was seen as a correct British standard—but it is now, in its basic structure, the same as in the early days of settlement.

There are also many myths about our accent—that we speak through our noses because we have to keep our mouths shut to stop the flies getting in, or, because our sinuses are swollen with hayfever from the dust and pollen and grass seeds that surround us. Nasality was a feature of the broad Australian accent, though it was an inherited feature and not acquired in the outback. Today, most Australians speak with a general or educated Australian accent.

After accent, it is the special words we use to describe our way of life that distinguish our English from others. This book explores the unique vocabulary of Australian English to reveal the ways in which English has adapted to a new country.

### new meanings for old words

The settlers of the late eighteenth century brought with them a mental world fashioned back in England and they attempted to classify their new physical world in line with their memory of Home. Indeed, one of the behaviours of homesick colonists was that they clung to their past with a fervour not matched by the society that they left. It came as a shock to British colonists who 'went Home' that 'Home' was no longer as they imagined it to be.

For the white settlers in Australia it was a natural reaction to try to reconstruct the society they had left behind, but they encountered resistance to this imposed pattern and the differences eventually became too strong to ignore. Words started to lose their original meanings and to acquire new ones forced upon them by circumstances. Take 'paddock', for example. Originally a small enclosure near the house, the concept of a paddock grew bigger and bigger until a paddock in Australia was equal to whole counties back in England. Words in this book that reveal a similar process of alteration are 'creek', 'bush', 'scrub', 'station'.

## invented words

Finding new words was the other language challenge that confronted the settlers. Again they looked to similarities with their past: a bird that looked like a pigeon became a 'native pigeon', a tree that had fruit that looked like a plum became a 'native plum'. But what to do with objects that didn't resemble anything at all? It is actually quite difficult to coin a brand new word.

The easiest and most successful method of making up new words in English is to form compounds, that is, to put two words together to make a new one that is more than the sum of the meanings of the two base words. A page of any English dictionary has many examples of this. One that caught my eye was 'fiddlesticks'. We know what it means to 'fiddle'. We know what 'sticks' are. Put them together and you have the game which children play. We rarely re-analyse these compounds into their component parts—the new meaning attaches to the whole word, but we can, if we stop to consider, see what thinking led to the combination word.

The development of word compounds can be particularly successful if one of the root words has special significance in terms of the culture. One such word used in this dictionary is 'bush'. This word has a special meaning and importance in Australian English and a whole cluster of compounds have grown from it including 'bush ballad', 'bushed', 'bush-bashing', 'bush jam tart', 'bush lawyer', 'bushranger', 'bush telegraph' and 'bushwalking'.

## borrowed words

There are only a little over 400 words borrowed from Aboriginal languages used in Australian English, so in terms of numbers this source is not significant. The words, however, are often highly visible ones—names of plants and animals and features of the Australian environment which we encounter again and again. This special set of words greatly contributes to the sense that Australian English is different from other Englishes.

A good number of Aboriginal borrowings come from the Port Jackson Aborigines, whose language was documented by officers of the First Fleet. Lieutenant William Dawes recorded words like 'wombat', 'wallaby', 'waratah', 'boomerang', 'corroboree' and 'cooee'—all of which were borrowed from the speakers of Dharug, or 'the Sydney Language'.

Other Aboriginal borrowings followed soon after from new settlements and other colonies. 'Budgerigars' were encountered by explorers as they crossed the Great Dividing Range. The 'coolabah' and 'nardoo' grew in inland Australia, the 'mallee' in Victoria, the 'mulga' in New South Wales and the 'quokka' and 'jarrah' were found in Western Australia.

In turn, the Aborigines borrowed English words and a variety of pidgin developed which formed the basis for Aboriginal English. In some instances English words that had arrived with the first settlers travelled from their first Aboriginal point of contact through pidgin and Aboriginal English, crossing from one Aboriginal community to another. 'Gammon' is one example of this method of dissemination.

## rhyming slang

Rhyming slang has been a continuing source of new words in Australian English since the 1800s. Much of the entertainment of rhyming slang (or 'Old Jack Lang') is in creating new rhymes, clear enough in context for listeners to understand the reference, but novel and creative enough to surprise them.

The path rhyming slang follows, however, is a predictable one. In the early stages the rhyme is new and startling and has to be given in full. A 'Noah's ark' is a 'shark'. Then the joke catches on to the point where it becomes fashionable to abbreviate the rhyme in the certain knowledge that just a hint is enough. A 'Noah's ark' becomes a 'noah's' and then a 'noah'. This shortened form becomes the preferred one and so people learn the term without any idea of its birthplace. The community loses its collective memory of the rhyme that started the joke and the word becomes a general item of colloquialism. To be 'on your pat' is to be 'on our own' or 'alone'. This was a rhyme on 'Pat Malone' who, by all accounts was a fictitious character—the joke being to create a person out of an ordinary word 'alone'. 'Onkaparinga', on the other hand, worked the other way round. There is a river in South Australia called the Onkaparinga, an Anglicisation of the Kaurna name. In time this became known as the trademark of a type of blanket and, as the blanket became better known, a rhyme with 'finger' appeared, and the name was shortened to 'onka'.

Many rhymes do not survive the conversation that generated them, although some do stick. A colonial cook was called a 'babbling brook' which was shortened to 'babbler'. Other names for a cook are much more telling—'poisoner', 'stiffener', 'baitlayer', 'dough puncher', 'greasy', 'gutstarver', 'water burner'.

In the streets of London rhyming slang was a coded language, a way of ensuring that what you were saying was not understood by outsiders. The coded word is therefore not connected by meaning at all and instead picks up on well-established collocations that will be familiar to the listener. The term 'china plate' was common enough, the rhyme with 'mate' a natural one, and the reduction to 'china' completed the process of mystification. Both 'china' and 'babbler' are thought to have started life as British military slang despite claims for an independent existence in Australian English.

## diminutive endings

The diminutive suffixes '-ie' and '-o' are not unique to Australian English, but the amount of work they do for us is seen as considerably different from that of other Englishes. *The Macquarie Dictionary* comments that '-ie' can be used as 'a sign of affection' ('kiddies'), a familiar abbreviation ('postie', 'pressie'), or as a functional way of turning an adjective into a noun ('greenie', 'littlie').

The suffix '-o' on the other hand probably began with the cries of street vendors who found that adding '-o' to the end of the commodity they were selling gave them something that would help carry the voice. Thus we have 'milk-o' and 'rabbit-oh'. The familiar Aussie 'smoko' came from the cry 'smoke-oh!' used to inform the workers that it was time for a break and a much needed cigarette. It is a small jump in meaning from the vendor's cry to the name for the vendor himself: 'milko' or 'rabbitoh'.

Other occupations and pursuits are treated in a similar way—'garbo', 'journo'—and from this we reach the point where any kind of distinctive feature can be turned into a noun through remarkably efficient stereotyping—'dero', 'plonko'.

The other line of development of the '-o' suffix is as a simple abbreviation—'arvo', 'commo', 'demo'. Here it serves the same function and overlaps with the '-ie' suffix. Why not 'arvie', 'commie', 'demmie'? Indeed, 'commie' does exist as an alternative; the phrase is 'commie bastard', not 'commo bastard'. A sense of language rhythm decides which works best in which context.

## regionalism

A regionalism is a word or phrase that is restricted to a particular locality. Such localism in Australia is evident in clusters of words which include names for classes and grades in school, names for foods and names for plants and animals. So we have 'area school' (SA), 'central school' (NSW), 'consolidated school' (Victoria), 'district school' (Tasmania). Where you were born can often be revealed in your language choices: 'bubbler' or 'drinking fountain', 'bidgee widgee' or 'buzzy', 'best and fairest' or 'fairest and best'.

There are two kinds of regionalism. There are instances where speakers must use a regional term because there is no word that is used all over Australia. The 'magpie lark' of

Victoria is, for example, the 'peewee' of New South Wales, and we must choose between the two. There is no common name for us to share. Usually there is a word used everywhere in Australia as well as the regional word: 'autotray' and 'traymobile' yet 'trolley' will cover either.

Some other examples of regionalisms are 'elevener' (NSW), 'little lunch' (Queensland), 'playlunch' (NSW), and 'recess' (Victoria). The weed with the brilliant purple flowers is called 'Paterson's Curse' in New South Wales and 'Salvation Jane' in South Australia. It is also known as 'Lachlan lilac', 'Murrumbidgee sweetpea', and 'Riverina bluebell'.

Just as we like to identify ourselves as Australians by the way we talk and the words we use, we also quite like to feel that there is a discernible difference between people from various states, that we can tell a Queenslander from a Melburnian, and so on. One of the surprising features of Australian English is that in its standard form it is remarkably uniform around the country. This is probably a result of the degree of people's movement around the country from colonial times, and the early introduction of channels of communication such as overland telegraph which exposed us all to a standard form. Perhaps regionalism is a self-fulfilling thing, that in the face of all this standardisation of our English we actively choose to introduce little differences. It is a matter of balance—we don't want to be uncomfortably different but we do want to assert a regional experience.

## Australian colloquialism

Do Australians swear more than most? I doubt it, although we do have a fine tradition of swearing that goes back to the colonial days of the bullocky, who was renowned for his untiring eloquence in this register of the language.

Australians have traditionally viewed with suspicion any outward signs that mark one person as being superior to another. In Australian culture Jack is as good as his master or, at least, it needs to seem that way. So whereas other cultures draw a clear line between formal and informal language and hold the line against introducing informal language into formal situations, Australians can sound pretty relaxed at all times. This is as true of prime ministers today as it was of station owners in colonial times. Such persistent informality leads us to think that we have more colloquialisms than anyone else. This is unlikely to be true.

Of course our slang is distinctive and has its own particular flavour. There is a good deal of black humour in it, born of colonial adversity. Much that was slang yesterday is standard today, so we find that 'plant' as it is used in the term 'road plant' has its origins in convict slang. Slang invigorates and enriches a language and is the well-spring of difference for our variety of English.

Much of the early language work of the colonists had to do with the physical environment and the naming of plants and trees, fish and birds and animals. As the new colonial society grew it had to find other words for its system of government, its politics, its architecture, its culture and way of life. Subtle layers were then added to the language construct. And so this process continues today when, as Australians, we balance the influence of the outside world against our sense of ourselves, our traditions and our unique history in this land.

# (Aa)

## acacia

Nearby ornamental trees and bushes were clotted with birds. Acacias exploded into blossom like tiny bomb-bursts.

David Ireland, *The Unknown Industrial Prisoner*, 1971.

The botanical name 'acacia' comes from the Greek word 'akei' meaning a thorn and referring to a plant called the 'Egyptian thorn'. The name was then generalised to a group of Old World plants with spikes of yellow flowers. The Burning Bush mentioned in the Bible is believed to have been an acacia. Australians have turned the botanical name into a common name for various trees and shrubs with the distinctive yellow flowers of the Mimosaceae. Sometimes we have mistakenly extended the name to plants of the *Cassia* genus as well. However familiar we are with the name 'acacia', it is the common name 'wattle' which is the iconic one, which has the fragrance of our history and the overtones of nationalism.

## acca

> NSW University market day…Intended for the whole community, not just for accas (academic persons).
> *Sydney Morning Herald*, 3 September 1982.

This abbreviation for 'academic' first appeared in *Meanjin* (Melbourne, 1977) in the title of an article by Ken Inglis, 'Accas and Ockers: Australia's New Dictionaries'. Whatever Inglis meant, the editor of *Meanjin* made his interpretation clear in a footnote which read: 'acca (slightly derogatory) 1 noun. An academic rather than an intellectual, particularly adept at manipulating trendiologies, usually with full scholarly apparatus. Hence 2, noun. A particularly sterile piece of academic writing.'

As a general abbreviation for 'academic' the term is still used, more by those outside universities for those inside them, with connotations ranging from neutral to that general disrespect that Australians have for intellectuals. It seems to be a blokey word—the likelihood of a woman referring to herself or others as 'accas' seems remote.

## aerialist

Of the aerialists, Geelong's sensationalist Gary Ablett got up there higher and more often than any other player on the field. In front or from behind, there was just no keeping Ablett on terra firma as he blitzed his way to nine great goals and the Norm Smith Medal for the best player in the Grand Final.

*Sunday Sun* (Melbourne), 1989.

'Taking a mark' is one of the key skills in Aussie Rules so an 'aerialist', someone who has the ability to get up there and pluck a mark out of the ionosphere, is highly valued. It is a term peculiar to the jargon of Aussie Rules.

The amiably derisive name 'aerial ping-pong' refers to the high marks and the forwards and backwards flow of a good footy game. It is thought of as a particularly New South Wales term, but may be on the way to becoming obsolete now that Sydney has its own local teams and is as obsessive about them as any Melburnian.

## Anzac

ANZAC—Contraction of Australian and New Zealand Army Corps.
ANZAC BUTTON—Makeshift for trousers' button.
ANZAC STEW—Foul water.

ANZAC WAFER—Hard and flavourless biscuit.
Gilbert H. Lawson, *A Dictionary of Australian Words and Terms*, 1924.

The men of the Australian and New Zealand Army Corps are remembered for their heroic deeds in World War I on Anzac Day. But there are other traces in our language of them and their wartime experience. The linguistic evidence reminds us of the grim humour that was part and parcel of the horror of war.

An 'Anzac button' was a nail used in place of a trouser button. 'Anzac soup' was shellhole water polluted by a corpse. 'Anzac stew' was an urn of hot water and one bacon rind, 'much appreciated in the Suez Canal zone', according to W. H. Downing's book, *Digger Dialects*. An 'Anzac wafer' was a hard biscuit supplied to the AIF in place of bread and described as 'one of the most durable materials used in the war'. All these are indications of that state of mind in which to laugh at what is most shocking is the only way to retain one's sanity, when to joke about death was the only luxury left to the living.

## Anzac biscuit

'The kettle's on the boil,' she said. 'The scones are hot. Come on in, do.' The kitchen was bright with fresh paint; the wood stove shiny black with polish. Jessie spread a starched cloth on the wooden table. They were

> pumpkin scones, and there were anzac biscuits as well.
> Hesba Brinsmead, *Longtime Dreaming*, 1982.

We all have a cupboard in the halls of nostalgia which is crammed with the food of our youth—the gramma pies and lemon butter, the coconut ice and lamingtons, the vegemite sandwiches and chocolate crackles. Thanks to the current fad for comfort food a number of forgotten delights such as bread-and-butter pudding and pumpkin scones are being recycled. Anzac biscuits have a special place because they are linked with a sense of privations during the war, of patriotic duty on the home front.

**apostle bird**

> Of that camp I remember the large wild violets,
> the sound of the creek on stones,
> the wind-combed grass, the tree-trunks
> wrinkled and grey like elephant-legs all round us;
> and those apostle birds, so rude to strangers,
> so self-possessed and clannish,
> we were glad when they flew away.
> Judith Wright, 'Apostle-Birds' in *Collected Poems*, 1962.

Colonial attempts to name the curious new birds of the Australian environment, when they were not borrowings from Aboriginal languages, ranged from the fanciful to the purely descriptive. The 'apostle bird', for example, was named because of its habit of going around in groups. The settlers counted twelve for each group which led to the association with the twelve apostles. More scientific counts specify seven to twelve. In a similar religious vein, the 'friar bird' was thought to resemble a monk, with its bald head. The 'dollar bird' and the 'diamond bird' each had those markings on their wings. And the 'mallee fowl' and the 'plains wanderer' were linked to their habitats. While the friar bird was described as saying clearly 'poor soldier' and 'four o'clock', the mopoke was thought to be saying 'more pork' . The ways of naming are indeed various.

## assignment system

> Major Vickers also prospered. He had always been a careful man, and, having saved some money, had purchased land on favourable terms. The 'assignment system' enabled him to cultivate portions of it at a small expense, and, following the usual custom, he stocked his run with cattle and sheep.
>
> Marcus Clarke, *For the Term of His Natural Life*, 1874.

At its best, the system of assigning convicts to work for settlers benefited all. The government no longer had the expense of maintaining the prisoner, the settler had virtually free labour, and the convict acquired skills which would be useful once he became a farmer himself. The success of the system depended on whether the person to whom the convict was assigned was a reasonable master or not. The term 'assigned' meant that the convict remained the responsibility of the government, so that in the case of any wrongdoing the master was not authorised to administer punishment. Instead, the convict was reported to the government authority. A convict could be removed from one master and reassigned to another at any time. Despite the considerable constraints of this master–servant relationship, the assignment system was fundamental to the early development of New South Wales.

## Australia

'My father and mother were Scottish born, and I am only Australian by birth.'

'And you'll speak the Austrian tongue at home; it is a good thing you learned Scotch in Scotland, though your speech has a very queer sound with it,' said my namesake.

'Not Austrian,' I said. 'Australian! Out of Europe altogether. In the biggest island in the world that used to be called New Holland, to the south-east of India in the South Seas.'

Catherine Helen Spence, *Handfasted*, 1879.

'New Holland' was the original name for Australia, this being a translation of the Latin name 'Nova Hollandia' given by Dutch navigators of the seventeenth century to the bit of the continent that they observed, that is, the top end. But there was a rival name for the continent which had first appeared in the early sixteenth century and that was 'Terra Australis', the southern land. While Governor Phillip set about describing the Aborigines as 'New Hollanders' and emus as 'New Holland cassowaries', Governor Macquarie preferred to take the Australian tack. In this he followed the explorer Matthew Flinders, who felt that because different people had discovered different parts of the continent it was not right to extend to the whole continent the name given by the Dutch to one particular part of it. He preferred the all-encompassing 'Terra Australis' or 'Australia'.

By 1820 Governor Macquarie's policy on this seemed to be generally known. While there are nostalgic references to New Holland throughout the 1800s, the name was obsolete by the turn of the century. As can be seen from the quote above, the confusion of 'Australia' with 'Austria' that sometimes happens in other parts of the world dates back a long way.

# (Bb)

**babbling brook**

> Babbling brook, babbler: a cook; Baden Powell: a towel;
> bag of fruit: a suit; barmaid's blush: a flush, as in poker;
> Barney Maguire: a fire; barrel of fat: a hat.
>
> John Meredith, *Learn to Talk Old Jack Lang*, 1984.

Rhyming slang is something that we associate with Cockney,
but it has had a life of its own in Australia, and 'babbling
brook' for 'cook' seems to have been an Australasian invention. I say 'Australasian' because it is part of New Zealand
English as well, largely because shearing teams and their cooks
followed a route that took them through the shearing sheds
of both countries. This term came into fashion in the
late 1800s and, in the way of rhyming slang, was shortened
to 'babbler'.

The babbler was not an up-market cook. He was the kind

of bloke that dished out lots of stewed tea, burnt meat and doughy desserts of doubtful nature. Other names for him were 'dough-puncher', 'poisoner', 'baitlayer', 'gutstarver', 'crippen' (after the murderer of that name) and 'greasy'.

**badger box**

> The dwellings occupied by the piners when up the river are of the style known as 'Badger-boxes', in distinction from huts, which have perpendicular walls, while the Badger-box is like an inverted V in section.
>
> *Papers and Proceedings of the Royal Society of Tasmania*, 1864.

When it came to naming plants and animals in colonial Australia, the white settlers had two basic choices—to take the name that the Aborigines used or relate the object to their own experience. So if a tree had fruit like a plum tree it became a native plum. If an animal looked like a porcupine it became a native porcupine. The term 'badger' was the Tasmanian name for the wombat. 'Wombat' is from the Dharug language around Sydney and became the established term on the mainland. A box is, in one sense, a hut or small house.

**bandicoot**

> They shouted, 'Hi, you with the melon!' to attract his attention, and set off running after him, and the Bandicoot, being naturally of a terrified disposition, ran for all he was worth.
>
> Norman Lindsay, *The Magic Pudding*, 1918.

In the case of the bandicoot the likeness was drawn to an Indian mammal, the name meaning 'pig-rat'. Early recorded enthusiasm for the bandicoot relates to its agreeableness as a dinner dish. In 1818 there is a traveller's reference to dining on a bandicoot and finding it 'of good flavour'. In a London magazine a few years later the bandicoot was described as being fatter than a rabbit and very fine eating. But then the farmers arrived, the growers of grain, and the bandicoot became a threat to the crops. It was seen as an animal somewhere between the rat and the rabbit in its ability to scratch for survival on poor terrain. And so we acquired such phrases as 'miserable as a bandicoot', 'poor as a bandicoot'. Even the bandicoot in *The Magic Pudding* is a cowardly, thieving kind of animal. I prefer John Hepworth's version of it: 'The Bandicoot is rather beaut. Neat and clean, No way a fool: Like a rat that's been to finishing school.'

'I've got a job for you and Henry afterwards,' their father said. 'I saw some smoke coming out of the chimney of King's hut. That would mean old Jim is back. What about taking him a butt of potatoes and a few swedes. It might stop the old reprobate from sneaking down to bandicoot some of ours?'

Barney Roberts, *Where's Morning Gone?*, 1987.

The 'bandicoot' is known for its habit of digging. Bandicoot holes are quite modest affairs, scarcely noticed unless you know what you are looking for, but they give the animal access to juicy roots. In colonial times one way of getting potatoes was to steal them, making surreptitious holes to get to the tubers while leaving the plant apparently undisturbed. So 'bandicoot' acquired a verb sense as in 'to bandicoot the potatoes', or 'to bandicoot the potato patch'.

In the mining context 'bandicooting' described the activities of those who picked over the mullock heap left by other miners. This use of the word combines the bandicoot's physical habit of digging with its stereotype as a survivor on lean pickings.

**banksia**

It was a big old banksia full of dead heads, the trunk and branches of the tree tortured into abominable shapes, full of dust and ugliness.

Patrick White, *Tree of Man*, 1955.

The name 'banksia' is meant to remind us of Sir Joseph Banks. The plant that it was originally applied to belonged to a New Zealand plant genus which now has the name 'Pimelea'. Forster and Forster, father and son, applied the name in 1776, in honour of Joseph Banks, to a species of pimelea that they found in New Zealand. The common name for this plant is the riceflower.

In the 1780s there were a number of naturalists who wanted to honour Joseph Banks by naming a plant after him. It was left to the younger Linnaeus to sort out the conflict between 'banksia' and 'pimelea'. He opted for 'pimelea' for the riceflower and 'banksia' for the bottlebrush. This nomenclature was published in 1781 and over-rode Forster and Forster. Linnaeus may have published after Forster and Forster but his publication had greater influence.

The person who has given the banksia its highest public profile was, of course, May Gibbs, with her stories about Snugglepot and Cuddlepie and the bad Banksia men.

## baobab tree

At the side of this street ancient baobabs, or boabs, of incredible girth act as shade trees. They are one of the features of Derby. Some would be a good twelve feet through, squat, bulging, like blowsy old matrons with enormous thighs and waist and truncated arms.

Caralie and Leslie Rees, *Spinifex Walkabout*, 1853.

The baobab tree is related to the African tree from which it derives its name. In *A Natural History of Egypt* published in 1592, this African tree was described with the comment that the name appeared to be from some central African language.

In the jargon of the Top End, 'baobab' is often shortened to 'boab'. The botanical name, *Adansonia gregorii*, is after the explorer Augustus Charles Gregory, who carved a message into the trunk of a boab by the Victoria River.

The baobab also goes by the name of 'bottle tree'. Descriptions of the tree liken it to bottles used for soda water, port wine, beer and old-fashioned ginger-beer. From all this emerges two quite different shapes. The baobab type of bottle tree resembles a bottle planted in the ground with foliage like some fantastic flower arrangement stuck in it. The bottle tree native to Queensland is trim and tidy at the base, swells alarmingly in the middle and then tapers at the top; it is also called the 'gouty stem tree'.

The name 'monkey bread tree' refers to the pith of this fruit. The gum of the tree is used to make a drink described as 'a desert substitute for lemonade'. The swelling in the bottle tree is caused by the large amount of water stored in the trunk, which is its protection against drought.

## barcoo rot

The diet was deficient in vitamins, of course. You'd get the Barcoo Rot—come up in great big sores all over you. You couldn't keep the food away from the flies so you'd get the Barcoo Spews too.

Wendy Lowenstein and Morag Loh, *The Immigrants*, 1977.

---

The major complaint of the Barcoo region was the 'Barcoo rot', described as ulcers that spread from any cut or scratch which wouldn't heal. These were caused by a chronic streptococcal skin infection, although colonial diagnosis was that it was a form of scurvy, a direct result of the common diet of bread and meat with no greens.

There was another complaint of the times that went by a variety of names—'Barcoo sickness', 'Burdekin vomit', 'Belyando spew'. It was a distinctive characteristic of the illness that sufferers vomited at the sight or even the thought of food. Two explanations were offered for it—bad water, and an unpleasant after-effect of being bitten by a species of fly. More recently the suggestion has been that the sickness was caused by cyanobacteria—the same blue-green algae that today increasingly signals problems in our stressed-out river systems.

## barney

> This bit of a barney, of course, made bad blood betwixt us and Moran's mob, so for a spell Starlight and father thought it handier for us to go our own road and let them go theirs. We never could agree with chaps like them, and that was the long and the short of it.
>
> Rolf Boldrewood, *Robbery under Arms*, 1889.

This is a piece of Yorkshire dialect that has taken a central place in Australian English. At the core of male society is 'the barney between two old bush mates that threatens to end up in a bloody fist-fight and separation for life, but chances to end in a beer'. So Henry Lawson said in his reflections on the barney as being central to the 'hearts of men in matters of man to man—of man friend to man friend'. The *English Dialect Dictionary* would seem to indicate that a barney had much the same social function in Yorkshire as it had in the Australian bush—a chance to let off steam and speak one's mind, which was stopped if it ever threatened to become serious.

## barra

> Smimac, local suppliers of 'barra, buff and roo' in Alice Springs, said satisfying the tourists' predilection for kangaroo cuts was keeping it busy.
>
> *Mercury* (Hobart), 1989.

If there is one fish that we would think of as a national dish then it has to be the barramundi, affectionately shortened to 'barra'. The name is thought to be borrowed from a Queensland Aboriginal language although it has not been definitely located. Naming fish is a slippery business as local customs vary so that a barramundi in one river is a lungfish in another. There are those that would argue that the fish incorrectly designated 'the barra' is the Fitzroy perch, and that the barra is strictly speaking the Queensland lungfish. With the name hooked to different fish the Australian government felt the need to standardise. In this tidy-up of nomenclature the name barramundi has gone to the food fish of northern Australia.

**barrack**

> Sydney has more than its fair share of roughs…They are larrikins, deadbeats, grass-chewers, louts; gangs of youths and young men who live how they can and where they can and take their fun as they find it. Their steadiest interest is spotting a winner. They watch games, though they neither play them nor understand them, and they speak their minds. They, principally, are the barrackers, whose jeers and horseplay spoil many a good match.
>
> Thomas Wood, *Cobbers*, 1934.

## barrack

In the Irish dialect from which this word comes, to 'barrack' was to boast or brag. 'Oh, he's only barracking' you would say of someone sounding off about their own abilities. In Australia this use shifted to jeering at someone else, as if, in this process of one-upmanship, rather than show your own strengths, it was more effective to have a go at the weakness of others. This was all done as a loud verbal display.

From there it is a small step to barracking for others—such as a team that you support. In its early days barracking involved much jeering at the opposition. The barracker yelled support from the sidelines, usually by casting aspersions on the ability, looks and ancestry of the opposition. These days barracking has lost the negative connotations of the quote above and mostly brings out the positive aspects of cheering on the team that the barracker supports, rather than heckling the other side.

## battler

His walk became a swagger. He would always help a lame dog over the stile, that was his boast. He had become quite a personality. 'Jack West has done well for himself,' most people said, paying grudging admiration to a battler who had got on yet was sympathetic and generous to the poor.

Frank Hardy, *Power without Glory*, 1950.

Unlike the true-blue Aussie, the 'battler' is still a significant figure in the array of Australian stereotypes available to us and one that politicians still invoke when they wish to be thought of as decent human beings. For people striving to make ends meet, in the city or the bush, the term had more meaning than it does today. The 'battler' displayed indefatigable courage under circumstances beyond the individual's control, often not so much for their own sake as for the sake of the lives which were dependent on them. The 'battler' acquired associated virtues of humility and integrity. These days the term can be used with a shade of condescension—the 'battler' has no skills and no future but they try hard.

## berley

> Fresh pilchards and strips of salmon, mullet and garfish are recommended. Berley will help as well. Crushed mussels in their shells are excellent, particularly if mixed with a little fish oil.
>
> *Sunday Herald* (Melbourne), 1989.

Any fisherman knows that the way to get the fish biting is to throw out the berley, that is, ground-up bait of whatever kind is available. There are some words in Australian English where finding the origin is going to be hard—words possibly from Aboriginal languages where the path into English is obscured. 'Berley', however, smacks of British dialect and yet cannot be found under any variation of spelling in any of the dialects that have so much influenced our variety of English. It is hard to admit that the best information we have is 'origin unknown'.

The noun has given rise to a verb as in 'to berley the water'. It has also a figurative use for any attempt to deceive or to put one over someone.

## billabong

You know what those billabongs are: dry gullies till the river rises from the Queensland rains and backs them up till the water runs round into the river again and makes anabranches of 'em—places that you thought were hollows you'll find above water, and you can row over places you thought were hills. There's no water so treacherous and deceitful as you'll find in some of those billabongs.

Henry Lawson, 'The Blindness of One-Eyed Bogan'
in *Send Round the Hat*, 1914.

Water has always been a precious commodity in Australia, and places where it can be found often have special names which have come to us from the Aborigines. The derivation of 'billabong' is obscure, but it may well have come from the Aboriginal word 'billa' meaning 'water', and '-bong', a word ending indicating that the river flowed only after rain.

For the Aborigines, this was the name of a specific river, a fact which explorer Thomas Mitchell recorded in his 1836 South Australian journal but went on to ignore in calling the waterway the Bell River. But the Aboriginal name was also known and was then applied to the remnants of rivers of this type, the waterholes which mark the course that a river might take after rain.

## billy

> We had our tools for prospecting,
> Tin dish, tea and billy,
> Fowling-piece, and all excepting
> Grub, which does seem silly…
>> H. Head, 'A Wild Goose Chase in the Whipstick
>> Scrub', date unknown.

Some words can barely manage to scrape together one etymology, others seem to be encumbered with a number of them. There have been various attempts at explaining the origin of 'billy', some of them quite ingenious. It was, for example, argued that travellers in the early days of settlement relied on a popular tinned meat which had the French label 'boeuf bouilli'. A shorthand reference to this was 'bouilli-tin' which became the anglicised 'billy'. Not true of course but an engaging explanation. Another idea was to relate 'billy' to the Aboriginal 'billabong', 'billa' meaning 'water'. Yet a third was that 'billy' was a shortened form of William, an affectionate name for a personified cooking utensil.

It seems clear now that 'billy' is a variant form of the Scottish dialect word 'bally', from 'bally-cog' meaning a milk pail.

## bindi-eye

Greedy suburban birds grow very tame, and their claws are impervious to 'bindis' (bindi-i is a burr that grows in grass).

Nancy Keesing, *Lily on the Dustbin*, 1982.

The experience of stepping on 'bindi-eyes' or 'bindis' is one that many Australians share. In the eastern states they are also known as jo-jos, and many people would be familiar with balancing on one foot while plucking out bindis from the other. 'Bindi-eye' is an Anglicisation of the Aboriginal word 'bindayaa' from the language of the Kamilaroi and Yuwaalarraay of the Namoi River district in New South Wales. The earliest record of its use was in 1896.

## blackbirding

They said Suderman was a 'loud-mouthed old bastard', and that although he claimed to have made his money pearling, he had really made it blackbirding natives from the Pacific Islands to the Queensland sugar-plantations.

Kylie Tennant, *Lost Haven*, 1946.

'Blackbird' was nineteenth-century American slang for an African slave. Capturing such slaves was referred to as 'black-bird catching' and extended from the coast of Africa to the islands of Melanesia. The term was transferred into the Australian context in the late nineteenth century to mean abducting Pacific Islanders and bringing them to work in the Queensland cotton and sugar plantations. The islanders were known as Kanakas, 'kanaka' being the Hawaiian word for 'a man'. Hard on the heels of Federation came the White Australia Policy and it was with this end in view that legislation was passed to remove all the Kanakas in Queensland, approximately 9000, and to put an end to this system of labour in the plantations.

## black stump

Half-an-hour before sundown we rode up to the Black Stump. It was a rum-looking spot, but everybody knew it for miles round. There was nothing like it anywhere handy...We all drew rein round the stump. It had been a tremendous big old ironbark tree—nobody knew how old, but it had had its top blown off in a thunderstorm, and the carriers had lighted so many fires against the roots of it that it had been killed at last, and the sides were black as a steamer's funnel.

Rolf Boldrewood, *Robbery under Arms*, 1889.

In colonial times trees served as markers on the landscape. A twist in the fence or a big stump were part of a terrain that was mapped, albeit in a rough and ready fashion. 'Beyond the black stump' you were in uncharted wilderness. 'This side of the black stump' was mapped and measured, so the claim that something was the best, the biggest or the fastest this side of the black stump was an emphatic way of claiming a record in the known world.

Over time people came to think that the phrase referred to a particular black stump. Supply followed demand and various towns, hotels and establishments claimed to be on the site of the original, mythical black stump.

**blind Freddy**

'So there she comes walking along the footpath and when she seen me she tried to hide what she was carrying but

blind Freddie could tell it was a bottle pushed down
into her shopping bag.'

Nancy Keesing, *Lily on the Dustbin*, 1982.

There are two suggestions as to who the original Blind Freddy
might have been. One is that it was a nickname for Sir
Frederick Pottinger, an inspector of police in the 1850s. He was
known for his incompetence, his most notable failures being
allowing the bushranger Frank Gardiner to escape (Pottinger's
gun misfired at the critical moment) and accidentally killing
himself (his gun went off in the carriage as he returned to
Sydney). Neither of these events involved blindness however.
The other explanation is that Freddy was a street hawker in
Sydney in the 1920s. The earliest recorded use is in the 1940s,
which favours the Sydney peddler. Whatever the origin, we still
regard blind Freddy as a measure of the painfully obvious.

## bloke

If blokeyness were a sound, it would be the *phhhft!* of
opening a beer.

*Good Weekend*, 29 August 1998.

No-one knows for sure the origin of the word 'bloke', but the
best guess is that it is from Shelta, the language of the gipsies,
and was the word for 'a man'. In British English it became
the word for a man who wielded some kind of authority.

For the convicts, and for newly settled Australia, 'the Bloke' was the man who ran the show, whether that show was a business in town or a cattle station in the bush. It was therefore important that 'the Bloke' should be a 'good Bloke', because otherwise people under his control might suffer. As a result qualities of fairness and decency became attached to the notion of a 'bloke' and it became a generalised term in Australian English for any man.

In the context of feminism the analysis of what makes a man a man was in a jokey way reduced to a single word—'blokiness'. (This word is new enough for there to be some debate about the spelling—'blokiness' or 'blokeyness'.) 'Blokey behaviour' was viewed as those things that men must do for the sake of their masculine self-image. Watching the footie on Saturday arvo while sharing a beer with your mates was quintessential 'blokey behaviour'. 'Bloke' may now be threatened by 'guy' or 'dude' in the lexicon of the younger generation, but it will never entirely die out in Australian English because neither 'guy' nor 'dude' has the kind of moral underpinning that supports the notion of 'a good bloke'.

**bludger**
On Monday when they arrived back Alf was still in the camp looking contented. The cook had fed him and

> the bludger wouldn't go away, not while there was free grub.
>
> Bluey, *Bush Contractors*, 1975.

Originally the 'bludger' was the lowest of the low because he was a man who lived on the earnings of a prostitute. He protected those earnings by his use of a bludgeon—'bludger' is a shortened form of 'bludgeoner'. Although 'bludgeoner' in this sense was known in the mid-1800s in British English, the specific meaning of pimp seems to have developed in Australian English and been current up to the 1950s. Over the course of the twentieth century the meaning was expanded to cover anyone who profited from the efforts of others. It can therefore be used as a general term of abuse.

The derogatory term 'dole bludger' first appeared in the 1970s to refer to a recipient of unemployment benefits who lives off the taxpayers.

## blue

> I came without a girl and though you've got your pick of sex-kittens it's really pretty limited except for the gate-crashers who usually roar round in souped-up cars, but they're generally toughs and us lesser toughs usually give them as wide a berth as they'll let you in case they bung on a blue.
>
> Dymphna Cusack, *Black Lightning*, 1964.

[27]

## blue

There are many meanings in the dictionary for 'blue' but one that is regarded as essentially Australian is the colloquialism for an argument. There is no clear evidence for the origin of this 'blue', but the best guess is that it is linked with blue language or swearing. The fact that our bad language is 'blue' rather than red or purple might date back to an eighteenth-century colloquialism in British English. 'To blue' was to blush, and 'to make someone blue' was to cause them to blush. In Philippine English, just to illustrate the vagaries of language, vulgar talk is described as 'green'.

It is not unknown for an argument to involve swearing so it seems logical that 'blue' should come to refer to the argument itself. From there it developed a verbal function—'to blue with someone' is to have an argument with them. While perfectly possible in linguistic terms, this verb does not seem to have as much currency as the phrasal form—'stack on' or 'bung on a blue with someone'.

## bluey

Father had humped his bluey in Queensland and was familiar with the ways of swagmen. He always called them 'travellers'. The bearded men who kept to the bush he called 'Scrub Turkeys' and those who came down from the plains he called 'Plain Turkeys'. He could tell the difference between them and whether they were broke or not.

Alan Marshall, *I Can Jump Puddles*, 1955.

'Blue' plus the nominal '-ey' ending gives you 'bluey' meaning 'swag'. The swagman's bundle was invariably wrapped up in the common blue woollen blanket made in Tasmania, the beauty of which was that it was not only warm but waterproof. In the 1960s, Sidney J. Baker noted in his book *The Australian Language* that this blanket referred to as 'the blue' was still being made in Victoria. The phrase to 'hump your bluey' was a lightning sketch of the figure that the swagman cut with the hump of the swag on his back. Baker also wrote that the swagman who was a pro used only two straps to tie his bluey—one at each end—whereas the rookie, who was not so adept at rolling the swag, sometimes succumbed to the weakness of using three, and instantly advertised his inexperience.

There is another sense of 'bluey' that is worth mentioning. There are those among us who always like to call a spade 'a spade', but there are others who follow a perverse and twisted path, who call black 'white' and white 'black', often in jest or playfulness. In the game of contraries, irony plays a major part, so that the nickname 'Shorty' could be given to someone who is either very short or very tall. Black may be the opposite of white, but for the other colours it is a bit difficult to decide what's what. Certainly Australians seem to feel that 'blue' is the opposite of red, and so the nickname for a redhead is 'Bluey' or 'Blue'. Maybe it works as a kind of verbal underlining, a way of highlighting the most obvious and noticeable thing about someone. This way of arriving at a nickname is common to English speakers around the world, though it seems that this particular name for redheads is linked to Australians and has been most popular here since the late 1800s.

### bobby-dazzler

'Marvellous game,' he said slowly. 'I could have kissed Dale when he came across with that field goal. Right from half-way, too. A bobby dazzler, no kidding.'

Frederick J. Thwaites, 'The Melody Lingers', 1935.

We owe this wonderful word of praise to the Yorkshire dialect but it has an honourable history in Australian English, so we can fairly lay claim to it as well. The story begins in the early 1800s with the dialectal use of 'dazzler' as something or someone of striking merit, an expression which worked its way into mainstream British English—Dickens used it in *Nicholas Nickleby* in 1838. But as is often the way with such expressions of approval, constant use makes them seem less impressive, so to beef up 'dazzler' it is linked with 'bob' (which, in combination, is more easily said as 'bobby'). 'Bob' in this sense is again dialectal and has the sense of 'surprising suddenness' as in 'full bob'. Later, when the colloquialism 'bobby' for a policeman was current, the word 'bobby-dazzler' was reanalysed and the variant 'ruby-dazzler' coined.

## bodgie

> He was the tallest of our mob, and also fairly well built.
> He had black wavy hair cut in a Tony Curtis style with
> a duck's tail and square neck-trim and it really suited
> him. He was an exceptionally good-looker and was a
> killer with the sheilas. He dressed quite well and was the
> perfect example of a true bodgie. He 'dug the crazy
> bodgie talk real well, man,' as he put it.
>
> William Dick, *A Bunch of Ratbags*, 1965.

In the 1950s and 1960s bodgies were the thing for young men
to be. The typical bodgie had long hair in a duck's tail at the
back, loud shirts, bracelets, and large jackets with tapering
drapes which gave the illusion of the wearer having incredibly
broad shoulders. Bodgies were the rebels, cool and hep, in a
jive decade. Their opposites were the 'squares', though not all
squares were 'jells' or cowards. The coppers were the enemy
because they picked on the bodgies. And the bodgies felt they
had every right to pick on the Dagoes, or any other immigrant
for that matter.

There are a couple of explanations for the word 'bodgie'.
The first is that the Americans derived it, possibly from a version
of 'boysies'. But there is no particular evidence that 'boysie' was
current in American slang generally, let alone jive talk. On the
other hand 'boysie' does appear in Australian English where
there is a rival claim that 'bodgie' is related to the word 'bodger'
meaning 'fake'. This colloquialism was popular in the 1950s and

[31]

turned up in a number of expressions such as 'bodgie boy', 'bodgie club', 'bodgie cult'. The idea was that if something bodgie was faked, someone bodgie was equally derivative, and bodgies were seen to be aping American styles.

The companion of the 'bodgie' was the 'widgie' which, while apparently formed from 'bodgie', is of origin unknown.


## bogan

> Bogan—noun: person wearing a lumberjack shirt, ugg boots and skintight black jeans.
>
> Student essay, University of South Australia, 1993.

One of the things teenagers fear is to be out of step with their peers, to be 'uncool' in some way. That elusive difference is often most clearly visible in clothing. Many words for the uncool person are imports from America, words like 'nerd' and 'dork', 'reject' and 'loser'. Our home-grown Australian word is 'bogan'. The origin is not clear but its widespread use came from the popular 1980s TV comic character Kylie Mole who defined a bogan as 'a person that you just don't bother with. Someone who wears their socks the wrong way or has the same number of holes in both legs of their stockings. A complete loser.'

## boilover

'Boilover—Favourites not winning. Bookmakers and sporting men out in their calculations.'

Anon, *The Detectives' Handbook*, 1882.

This Australian colloquialism originated on the track but has now become common currency in sporting language. It refers to a situation in which the horse or team or player expected to win is beaten by a rank outsider. 'Boilover' in the racing context dates back to the mid-1800s but more recently there is 1960s evidence of its use in cricket and football commentary. Why the cooking metaphor? My guess is that it follows another Australianism, 'to cook something up' meaning 'to make something happen to your advantage'. From the punters' point of view at the racetrack they have something cooking on the favourite but then the unexpected happens—the boilover.

## bombo

He was so far gone down the path to physical and mental ruin that no one had the heart to refuse him a drink when he came begging for one; anything came well to the Kidger, plonk, plink, metho, bombo, or just ordinary whisky.

Ruth Park, *Poor Man's Orange*, 1949.

'Bombo', meaning 'cheap wine', has a history that stretches back into British English. It was first recorded in that variety in 1748 as a kind of weak punch and came from the Italian 'bombo', a child's word for a drink.

There is a rival theory that the word was independently coined as a combination of 'bomb' plus '-o'. The 'bomb' in Australian slang is an old, unreliable motor car and by extension, anything that is useless or of inferior quality. While there is much evidence for our use of 'bomb' for a car, there is, however, none for 'bomb' as cheap wine. So the connection is unproved. On the other hand, the link between watered-down punch and cheap wine seems quite logical.

If this word is a hand-me-down from British English then it seems to have been part of our World War II experience—the first citation for the word in Australian English dated 1942 says that it has become the 'in' word for cheap wine, replacing 'plonk'.

## bombora

When the waves surge in under the golden arch of basalt at Diamond Head, between the ledges dripping with weed and cunjevoi, you can hear the boom from the cliff-top with the surge of the bombora and the boom again.

Kylie Tennant, *The Man on the Headland*, 1971.

A 'bombora' is a wave that breaks offshore over a submerged reef. The size of the wave varies with the tide, at times being an unbroken swell, at others an apparently inexplicable surf. It is thought that 'bombora' might have been the Dharug name for a current off Dobroyd Head in Port Jackson. Today the term refers to any such wave formation of which there are a number, usually close to cliffs. 'Bomboras' are a trap for the unwary and are dangerous, so the word has been used figuratively in the same sense as 'whirlpool' or 'maelstrom'. Surfers, however, regard them as a good source of waves.

## bonzer

A note of enthusiasm crept into Bob's voice. 'I live at Murrumbeena myself. I've got a bonzer little joint not ten minutes from the station.'

John Morrison, 'No Blood on Deck' in *Stories of the Waterfront*, 1947.

This word is a colloquialism, that is, part of the spoken language, and its written form is the result of that oral honing. The starting point is the French word 'bon' meaning 'good' which in the English slang of the late 1800s was emphasised by the ending '-ster'. As an early commentator remarks, something that is 'bonster', surpasses something that is merely 'bon'. 'Bonster', however, is an unwieldy consonant cluster and was reduced to 'bonser', and then to 'bonzer', sometimes 'bonza' (possibly influenced by the spelling of 'bonanza'). Until World War II this was a powerful word in Australian English but after that we internationalised, and the city and the bush went their separate ways, much as they had done at the end of the 1800s. You will still find people who use 'bonzer' in the bush but for those in the city it is regarded as an Australianism that won't travel.

## boofhead

> Clearing his throat on the footpath he passed a pound note through the window to Shadbolt, and winked. 'Have a swim, give that boofhead of yours a bit of sun, take yourself off to the pictures. We've got a heavy programme tomorrow…'
>
> Murray Bail, *Holden's Performance*, 1988.

This word first appears in the 1940s when 'Boofhead' was the name of a comic strip character in the Sydney newspaper the *Mirror*. Australians have always enjoyed a light-hearted dig at their mates and friends, and 'boofhead' is a fine example of this type of friendly insult. 'Fathead', 'meathead' and 'bullet-head' are all similar insults and we are all familiar with the words 'fat', 'meat' and 'bullet', but just what is a 'boof'?

Well, nothing really. If there ever was a meaning of 'boof' it is now lost in time. One theory is that 'boofhead' is a shortening of an earlier insult, 'bufflehead'. That this was once used in Australia is attested to in the writing of Norman Lindsay. It comes from English dialect, meaning, literally, 'bullock head', since 'buffle' was an old term, borrowed from French, for a bullock.

## boomerang

Mr Askin's audience, a luncheon of the American Chamber of Commerce in Australia, clapped and cheered. Mr Askin said it was appropriate that the Chamber's coat of arms was a map of the US and Australia linked by a boomerang. The boast boomeranged on Askin. The outcry was intense, angry. The flustered Premier began calling it a 'little joke', a 'half-jocular remark,' not to be taken seriously.

Suzy Jarratt, *Permissive Australia*, 1970.

While much Aboriginal culture was hidden from or overlooked by white settlers, the boomerang was not to be ignored. Its shape, its flight, its function, all made it an item that was ripe for linguistic exploitation. In particular, the flight away and then back to the thrower was an image that could be applied metaphorically in many different contexts.

**boomerang**

There is some skill involved in catching the returning boomerang which would otherwise deal with the thrower as effectively as it dealt with the target, and so a certain amount of anxiety is associated with its return. What comes back to you is as likely to be unpleasant as not. One instance of a 'boomerang' is a bounced cheque. While this use has established itself in Australian English, there are examples of a wider use in more ad hoc circumstances, such as in references to a joke 'boomeranging' in a biter-bit style, and a voice 'boomeranging' as an echo. One further use, which is well established in the oral tradition, is the polite indication to a borrower that the lender expects the item to be returned, with the phrase, 'This is a boomerang, you know.'

**boronia**

The bush colours were in monotones, elegant and sophisticated. Small native rose plants, pink boronia bushes and tiny ground orchids were grouped about each wind-smoothed rock outcrop or shaggy trunk, in arrangements that landscape artists delight in.

Hesba Brinsmead, *Longtime Dreaming*, 1982.

A 'boronia' was among the early plant specimens sent back to the English botanist Sir James Smith. It was while he was considering these that Smith heard from his friend Dr

Sibthorp, who was studying plants in Greece, that Sibthorp's much valued assistant, the Italian botanist Francesco Borone, had fallen from a window and died. This accident was attributed to the after-effects of a fever. In honour of his friend's colleague, Sir James dedicated a genus to Borone describing him as 'a martyr to botany'. Thus are small histories recorded in the words we use.

Botany and zoology have a long tradition of turning names into memorials. There is 'Bennett's wallaby' and 'Bennett's tree kangaroo' named after George Bennett (1804–93), an Australian physician and naturalist; 'Sturt's desert pea' and 'Sturt's desert rose', named after the explorer Charles Sturt; the macadamia named by botanist Ferdinand von Mueller after John Macadam (1827–65), the secretary of the Philosophy Institute of Victoria. This is to name but a few.

## bowyangs

The days of the kangaroo, emu and noble bushman image of Australia were drawing to an end. The President of the Arts and Crafts Society in Melbourne, Professor Baldwin Spencer, has told his members all those emblems must go—the kookaburra, the kangaroo, the emu and the wattle. They belonged to the age of the bowyang and the sliprail.

Manning Clark, *A History of Australia*, 1968.

## bowyangs

The bowyang is a forgotten symbol of colonial life, more particularly, of the bush labourer. Picture him in his blue-flannel singlet, moleskin trousers, neckerchief, slouch hat, belt, bowyangs and hobnail boots. The bowyangs were the leather straps that he used to hitch up his trousers below the knee so that the bottoms wouldn't get encased in mud. The poorest extemporised version of a bowyang was a piece of string.

Farm labourers in Britain had worn leather leggings which in the Lincolnshire dialect were called 'bowy-yanks', that is, yanks or leggings which were bowy or curved. The variant form 'boo-yangs' was also known in northern dialects along with the Scottish 'nickie-tams'.

The bowyang had sufficient cultural significance to give rise to characterisations of the bushman such as Ben Bowyang created by C. J. Dennis, and Bill Bowyang who wrote a weekly ballad for the *North Queensland Register*.

## boundary rider

Here and there we came on a lone boundary rider, living with his horse and his dog in a remote hut, visited once a month by the ration cart, with a month every year back in civilisation.

Harold Lewis, *Crow on a Barbed Wire Fence*, 1973.

From 1790, the year that, in an effort to improve agriculture, Governor Phillip issued allotments of land to ex-convicts, the notion of the boundary line became part of the fabric of life on the land. Initially, the boundary was identified by natural markers like creeks or mountain ridges, or by trees daubed with white paint. Then the fences went up. In the larger properties it was impossible to keep an eye on the fences on a casual basis, and so the job of the 'boundary rider' was created. These men rode day after day, repairing the fences, keeping their stock in and putting unwanted stock out.

In modern times the boundary rider of the bush has become the sports journalist of the Aussie Rules game who roams the line reporting the play and doing interviews.

## brickfielder

One afternoon of deepest summer, when a brickfielder was blowing, and the hideous native trees were fiendish, and the air had turned brown, Mrs Bonner developed a migraine...

Patrick White, *Voss*, 1957.

In Sydney in the 1830s the afternoon southerly, known for its squally nature as the 'southerly buster', blew straight in over Brickfield Hill, the site of the brickworks. An unfortunate consequence of this was that the wind brought with it a great deal of dust. James Backhouse, the naturalist, writing in the

1830s, complained of 'small pebbles pelting like rain, and clouds of red dust, formed, not however entirely from the brickfields, but also from the reddish sand and soil in the neighbourhood'.

In other parts of Australia a brickfielder is a hot wind rather than a cool one, but always one that is full of dust, usually blowing in from the desert. In many instances the dust is red, the colour of bricks. And even in Sydney, as soon as the old brickworks disappeared, 'brickfielder' came to be used to describe a hot westerly full of red dust.

### brigade

We had a generous lick of early summer last week and daylight saving starts at the end of this month to my delight and the irritation of the faded-curtains brigade.
*Mail* (Adelaide), 1989.

The Australian use of the word 'brigade' has produced many amusing combinations and can still be relied on for further invention. Behind the jocular use is the standard meaning of the word, a group of men united for some common purpose and often dressed in some kind of uniform.

In this sense we go from the 'army brigade' to the 'fire brigade' and from there to the 'midfield brigade' in a game of football and the 'kitchen brigade' in a big restaurant. But what lies beyond? The 'dressing-gown and slipper brigade', the 'white-shoe brigade', the 'faded-curtains brigade', the 'handbag brigade' (and for those who might think this is a reference to women, it is an Aussie Rules term equivalent to 'cream puffs' and 'sissies'). The irony lies in the contrast between the seriousness of the word 'brigade' and the levity of the qualifying adjective.

## brindabella

Most sheep-barbers either drink one or two bottles of beer between knocking-off and going in to tea or slap a brace of rums down. The last 'run' of the day is traditionally called 'The Rum Run'. Some go for the 'brindabella'—rum with a beer-chaser.
*Bulletin*, 1959.

The 'run' was a period of work in the day of a shearer. The brindabella has also been described as a drink made of rum and beer. Whether the two were mixed in the same glass or followed in succession, the combination was known by shearers under that name.

The Brindabellas are a mountain range near Canberra and so a feature of the landscape in the surrounding sheep country. A shearer looking to name his drink need only lift his eyes to find inspiration.

**brumby**

> Over the river by gravel and gum
> To a thunder of hoofbeats, hard-driven they come
> A host of young horses, and riders who sway
> Like a reed to the wind, and are round and away,
> When they find that the brumby has broken again
> To challenge their whips to the width of a plain.
>
> E. R. Murray, 'Young Horses', 1955.

The brumby is to Australia what the mustang is to America. There can be no doubt that these wild horses are seen as significant in our imaginings of bush culture. There is some debate about the origin of the word. There is the story of Lieutenant Brumby of the New South Wales Corps, who had always been interested in livestock and who imported some good horses while still serving in the army. In 1804 he was to sail for a new settlement in Tasmania. In preparation for the move, however, he had been unable to muster his horses which were, as a result, allowed to run wild. One always has to be suspicious of stories like this but there are a few points of confirmation. Brumby's interest in horses continued so that when he settled in Port Dalrymple he continued to breed, race, and import horses. And this story is strong in his family tradition. The alternative explanation is that it is a borrowing from an Aboriginal language, possibly from southern Queensland or northern New South Wales, that as yet has not been tracked down. Or that it came from the Irish 'bromach' meaning 'colt'.

## brummy

He's a real zany dealer this bastard. He's trying like crazy to pay us in shares from some brummy mine he's got (mind you it actually pays a divvy each year by the books, but I ain't pre-disposed to hang around for next year's divvy on ours).

Bluey, *Bush Contractors*, 1975.

In the early 1900s 'brummy' was a slang term that meant 'counterfeit'. The *Bulletin* in 1921 remarked that 'a dinkum coin rang true when thrown down, whereas a brummy fell with a thud'. The term is a shortened form of 'Brummagem' which was the popular name for the town of Birmingham in England. In the late 1600s there was a racket in counterfeit groats which had its base there. From this it followed that a counterfeit coin was a Brummagem. In Australia this was shortened to Brummy, perhaps because of a tendency towards such diminutives in slang and perhaps because the link with Brummagem had become obscure. The adjectival use followed and was broader, to cover anything that wasn't quite right.

## buckjump

There was buckjumping blood in the brown gelding's
veins,
But, lean-headed, with iron-like pins,
Of Pyrrhus and Panic he'd plentiful strains,
All their virtues and some of their sins.

> Harry Morant ('The Breaker'), 'Who's Riding
> Harlequin Now?', c. 1890s.

It was a common observation that colonial horses were not
as easy to ride as the horses in England. One particularly
nasty way that horses had of dislodging a rider was to jump
up in the air with the feet drawn together and the back
arched. This vicious habit was attributed to the fact that
horses ran wild in their early years and were then imperfectly
broken in and educated for riding. The way that they jumped
in the air was thought to resemble the way that a buck kangaroo would leap in the air when startled, thus the term
'buckjumper'.

## Buckley's chance

He wheeled his team on the mountainside and set 'em
a merry pace,
A-galloping over the rocks and stones, and a lot of
Boers gave chase;

> But Driver Smith had a fairish start, and he said to the
>     Boers, 'Good day,
> You have Buckley's chance for to catch a man that was
>     trained in Battery A.'
>> A. B. (Banjo) Paterson, 'Driver Smith' in
>> *Collected Verse*, 1902.

The expression 'You've got Buckley's' is going to require a lot of explanation for future generations of Australians. To start with, it is a joke, and jokes, once they reach a certain age, are heavy going. First, you have to tell the story of William Buckley, the convict who escaped from Port Phillip and, unbeknown to the white settlers who had given him up for dead, lived with the Aborigines from 1803 to 1835, at which point, much to everyone's astonishment, he reappeared. Buckley had no chance of survival, so people said. It turned out that he did have a chance—a very remote one, but one that worked in his favour.

For the second part of the story we move to prosperous Melbourne and the store 'Buckley and Nunn'. Some devastating wit decided that there was a joke to be made from the name, that it represented the two chances that Buckley had—'Buckley's chance' and 'Nunn' (none).

'Buckley's chance' therefore came to mean a 'remote chance', the alternative being no chance at all. Now that the store has disappeared, the phrase has cut its moorings and sails on like a ship with a burden of meaning but no ties to its past and its origin.

## budgerigar

Parrots like green and crimson flowers walking and chittering among the branches of the old silver-leaf ironbark down by the slip-rails. A flung shower of gems when the budgerigars, migrating, swirled up suddenly from the tall grasses of the gully.

Frank Dalby Davison, 'The Crown Lands Ranger' in *The Wells of Beersheba and Other Stories*, 1933.

---

This name was established by the late 1800s after many previous attempts at anglicising the Aboriginal word which produced such forms as 'betcherrygah', 'betshiregah', 'boodjerigah', and 'budgery garr'. The Aboriginal language from which the name is taken is Yuwaalaraay, spoken near Lightning Ridge in New South Wales, and there is a suggestion that the 'budgery' element meant 'handsome'. By the 1930s the budgerigar had become a favourite as a pet and its name was affectionately reduced to 'budgie'.

## bunyip

The pool was bottomless, and under the dark water there were bunyips, or perhaps only one bunyip, that had been there always. No one knew what a bunyip was, but it had been there before there were any white men, before Aunt Rosa's and Aunt May's father had

[48]

claimed the Pool, and it was the oldest thing in Australia.

Randolph Stow, *The Merry-Go-Round in the Sea*, 1965.

---

The 'bunyip' is a mythical creature—large, black and amphibious, and thought to live in waterholes. The word is easily traced back to the Wembawemba language of western Victoria, though there are many explanations for the creature and its supposed powers. One is that the bunyip is a tribal memory of the diprotodon, a very large marsupial that lived in swamps and waterways many millennia ago. Another is that the imaginary creature of the billabongs that excited the nervous imaginations of white settlers was in fact a very real and totally unthreatening animal.

People have, on occasion, claimed to have seen the bunyip and given lurid descriptions of it only to find that it was a musk duck in full display. Birds making unusual sounds in the night seem to have spooked quite a few travellers, the brown bittern in particular startling people with its booming night call.

These days the bunyip seems to have been emasculated, in white culture at least, to the point where it vies for advertising space with the Easter bilby, that Australian cousin of the Easter Bunny.

## Burdekin duck

> The northern species of waterfowl are nomadic within
> the tropical zone but rarely leave it. They include the
> magpie-goose, green pigmy goose, white-quilled pigmy
> goose, Burdekin duck, grass whistling duck, and water
> whistling duck.
>
> *The Encyclopedia of Nature*, 1998.

The splendid name 'Radjah sheldrake' was given by the
French physician and naturalist, Prosper Garnot, to the bird
which he saw in his travels in 1828 along the northern coast
of Australia. It is more mundanely referred to as the 'Burdekin
duck', by association with the Burdekin River in northern
Queensland. This common name is functional, if not melliflu-
ous or inspiring.

The epithet 'radjah' was meant to imply that this was a
handsome bird, an exotic aristocrat among ducks, with its pure
white head, neck and chest, and its rich chestnut back and
black tail.

'Sheldrake' is a word that goes back in its elements to
Middle English, the language of Chaucer, when, in the form
'sheldedrake', it meant literally 'a variegated or piebald drake'.
'Sheld' meant 'particoloured'. Our 'sheldrake' is of the same
genus, *Tadorna*, as its English cousins. The spelling 'radjah' is
an example of the process of fossilisation—a now obsolete
spelling of 'rajah', current at a time in which English was
experimenting with a number of different spellings for this

word until finally settling on 'rajah'—forever preserved in the standard name of this bird.

At another level of language, Burdekin duck is a colloquialism for corned beef, in the same way that colonial goose was in fact mutton.

## burl

> Trucks nudged for space at the gutters or burled along the reddish roads...
>
> Coralie and Leslie Rees, *Spinifex Walkabout*, 1953.

In Scottish English the word 'birl' means 'to make a noise like something revolving rapidly', which makes it likely that the word is onomatopoeic—like 'whirl' and 'twirl' and the like. This sense of movement is quickly transferred to the source of the movement. In Scottish English 'burl' becomes the name for 'a policeman's whistle' and the spinning wheel is 'the burling wheel'. Someone is said 'to burl along' when they depart at speed. And a coin 'burls' when it is spun in the air.

In Australian English we are left with the verb 'to burl along' and the phrase 'give it a burl'. This latter idiom probably relates to the 'burling' of a coin in games of chance. The earliest citation we have for the expression is from New Zealand in 1917. It mentions pennies being thrown up and burling well, with the onlookers crying 'Fair burl!', for which the more commonly known expression is 'Fair go!' The phrase 'give it a burl' still has that idea behind it of trying your luck. It may work, it may not, but you might as well give it a go.

## bush

All that country, which remains in a state of nature uncultivated and uninclosed, is known among the inhabitants of the Australian colonies by the expressive name of the bush.

W. Pridden, *Australia, Its History and Present Condition*, 1843.

---

It may come as a surprise to realise that this word, which we regard as one of the cornerstones of Australian English, is not of our own making. It entered English from the Dutch 'bosch' through South African English, and from there moved into American English. This established use for rough uncultivated terrain extended thereafter to the Australian landscape.

## bush ballad

The story told how the apple seeds had been brought from England to Australia by the first Alec Grey. He had crossed the mountains with his wife and had settled in the valley. There was a bush ballad about him and stories of his ghost being seen near a convict bridge.

Hugh Atkinson, *Grey's Valley: The Legend*, 1986.

You think of the 'bush ballad' and you think of Banjo Paterson and Adam Lindsay Gordon. This was a colonial genre of poetry perfected by such writers. It had great appeal to most Australians who, by the end of the 1800s, were largely living in cities and dreaming of life in the bush. This dream was fed by writers such as Henry Lawson and Steele Rudd, who were largely responsible for shaping the symbols that became the buzzwords for Australian culture—'wattle', 'mateship', 'fair dinkumness' and, above all, 'the bush'. Occasionally they believed in their own propaganda to such a degree that they took trips to the outback to get 'local colour', returning with barely disguised relief to the 'bohemian' life of the city.

## bush-bashing

27th July 1967. Writing on knees before take-off for the search for Gibson. 'If we find him will we take the remains to Alice for Christian burial?' Larry asks with a throw-away grin…The same evening. Some of the heaviest bush-bashing we've done to date. Charging

repeatedly at sand-ridges—ten attempts before we
breasted one. Many flat tyres.

Dal Stivens, *A Horse of Air*, 1986.

This is a simple concept for those with a simple approach to
life. Find a starting point in the bush, point yourself in the
direction of the spot you want to end up at, and blunder
through the bush until you get there. The blundering can be
on foot or by motor vehicle; with the popular fashion for
four-wheel-drives, something that was once done as part of
working life in the bush is now done by way of entertainment.

The 'bush-bashing' of settlement days referred to clearing
land of timber and was also called 'scrub-bashing' or
'sucker-bashing'. A 'bush-basher' went along and knocked the
suckers off trees which had been ringbarked. A follow-up
activity was 'emu-bobbing' which involved a team of men walking
slowly over the cleared land picking up the litter of wood and
branches. In more contemporary contexts the 'emu parade' is the
group of people detailed to pick up litter in a school yard or
camping ground. The image is the same—a group with heads
down and tails up, looking very much like a flock of emus.

## bushed

Four times that night they lost the track. 'It's like life,'
said the driver. 'We must go on although we get bushed

now and again.' 'But we'll get there,' answered Sister cheerfully.

Ion L. Idriess, *Flynn of the Inland*, 1932.

There are those who maintain that there is a subtle distinction between being 'lost' and being 'bushed'. According to this theory you are 'lost' when someone has to come and find you, but 'bushed' is when you have temporarily strayed from the path. In time you get your bearings, recognise a landmark, stumble onto a path you know, and set out confidently again.

Being 'bushed' can be a mental state as well as a physical one. If you are totally confused, if you can't get your mental bearings, then you are indeed bushed. One other meaning of 'bushed' is to be 'exhausted', but this is an Americanism that we have acquired.

### bush jam tart

Luscious bush jam tarts in tin plates, the jam ingeniously concocted of brown ration sugar and water.

J. C. F. Johnson, *Christmas on Carringa*, 1873.

The jam tarts referred to here are, of course, not the real thing. In more recent times they might have been referred to as Clayton's tarts. But in the 1870s 'bush' fairly frequently prefaced the makeshift and ad hoc creations that had to serve when the real thing was not available. 'Bush bread' was another name for damper. 'Bush champagne' was methylated spirits and saline.

This use of 'bush' was similar to the earlier use of 'Botany Bay', as in 'Botany Bay greens', the name given to a whitish velvety plant found to be edible in the early days of settlement. The description 'colonial' served the same function, as in 'colonial goose', the name given to a leg of mutton.

## bush lawyer

Swaine threw the fly back and stepped threateningly inside…

'Hold it there,' Dusty said.

Swaine stopped, looked hard at him. 'Hold what?'

'This is my house. You can't just bust in here for no reason.'

Swaine's eyes narrowed. 'So, a bush lawyer…'

Wal Watkins, *Andamooka*, 1971.

The 'bush lawyer' is someone who is willing to stand on his rights by argument rather than by force. A 'bush lawyer' can argue that black is white and white is black, so the gift of the gab is a prime requisite. Yet true 'bush lawyers' are more than just gifted orators; they manage to spice their rhetoric with the flavour of the law courts. They make it clear that they are arguing a case by employing a few legal terms.

Although you know that their knowledge of the law is no better than your own, in the uncertain light of the campfire, you can almost see the wig and gown.

## bushranger

'Fancy,' said Mrs Bonner with sudden animation, 'a short time ago a gentleman and his wife, I forget the name, were driving in their brougham on the South Head Road, when some man, a kind of bushranger, I suppose one would call him, rode up to their vehicle, and appropriated every single valuable the unfortunate couple had upon them.'

Patrick White, *Voss*, 1957.

'Bushranger' seems to be one of our first borrowings from American English and dates back to the early days of settled Australia. In American English the word had more positive connotations, the equivalent of our 'bushman', and describes someone who is good at ranging the bush and capable of surviving in it. In America, a 'bushranger' might well have been a pioneer, in Australia he was more than likely to be a convict who had 'absconded into the woods'. But with the gold rush of the 1850s, bushrangers blended with highwaymen and started bailing up the coaches, thereby establishing themselves in the folklore of the country.

## bush telegraph

'I was just coming along to your office to give you this. From Roy and me. The bush telegraph tells us that you and that gorgeous great Dutchman have gone and— well, that you're doing things properly. Well, good on yer, Ray. And the best of everything. You certainly deserve it, doll. Both of you.'

Neville Jackson, *No End to the Way*, 1965.

The original 'telegraph' was a member of a bushranger's gang whose job was to relay messages about such important events as the arrival of a mail coach or the presence of the troopers. This meaning evolved from a convict use of the word for the system of communicating among fellow prisoners. It was therefore necessary to specify that this was 'the *bush* telegraph', the unofficial system for getting information circulating in the vast open spaces of the bush. The bush telegraph, while respectable, was not altogether reliable, being one part information to nine parts gossip.

## bush tucker

Fitzer could tell plenty about living on bush tucker— lily-roots, crocodile-eggs, plains turkeys, and echidnas, or native porcupines.

Coralie and Leslie Rees, *Spinifex Walkabout*, 1953.

The word 'tucker' meaning food is from the early 1800s British schoolboy slang 'tuck in' meaning to eat greedily. Thus schools had tucker shops or tuckshops, though these days they more commonly have canteens. And the dog sat on the tucker box in which the food was stored. Bush tucker differs from ordinary tucker in that it is drawn from what is available in the bush. It implies dependence on the knowledge of the Aborigines for what is in season, for how to gather and prepare it. Though a colonial expression, it has gone up-market in recent years with restaurants specialising in it and TV programs giving it a high profile.

## bushwalking

If you have not rested at dusk and cooked a meal over a scented fire of gum-sticks and yarned and sung songs around the fire—if you have not done these things, you have not entered into your heritage as a true Australian.
Paddy Pallin, *Bushwalking around Sydney*, 1959.

Bushwalking seems to have been always part of the Australian way, but recreational walking dates back to the turn of the century and the term 'bushwalking' itself did not appear until 1927. There was some competition from other rival terms— the American 'hiking' and the British and New Zealand 'tramping'. Indeed, there was some debate about what exactly constituted bushwalking. Serious walkers scorned those people who, caught up in the American craze for hiking, headed out into the wilderness with no equipment, not even proper shoes, to commune with nature. Mountain trails demanded more respect. To some people at the time the combination of 'bush' and 'trail' smacked of Africa, since 'bush' was as much a part of the African landscape as the Australian, and 'trail' was a term used in Africa and America. So in 1927 the Bush Walkers Club was formed as a rival to the existing Mountain Trails Club. 'Bushwalking' has won out over 'trailing' as the preferred term, but there is still an echo of the debate over 'trails' versus 'tracks' to this day.

## bush week

Some lazybones, who compounded their sins by being cheeky, when asked 'What do you think this is? Bush Week?' will answer back, 'Yes, and you're the sap!'

Nancy Keesing, *Lily on the Dustbin*, 1982.

'Bush Week' was an occasion in the early 1900s when the bush came to town and for a week paraded its wares and lifestyle for the education of Sydney city slickers. Sadly it is not fixed in Australian culture as a time of enlightenment and understanding but as an opportunity for the city slickers to con, hoodwink and generally put one over the country visitors. The rhetorical question 'What do you think this is—bush week?' really means 'Do you take me for an idiot that you can scam?'

# (Cc)

## cactus

His high spirits descended temporarily. 'It took me thirty minutes to get her going again. The lift pump is cactused.'

Daryl Guppy, 'Some Days Are Rocks' in *Bundle of Yarns*, 1986.

---

Australian English has a number of expressions for being in the outback or in difficult terrain which specify the type of vegetation—'in the mulga' is one. A variation on this theme, 'in the cactus', emerged in the 1940s. World War II soldiers gave a figurative sense to this as a slang expression 'in the cactus' meaning 'in trouble'. By extension, something that had been in the cactus could then be described as 'cactus' or 'ruined'. The verb 'to cactus' produced the past participle 'cactused'.

An alternative explanation for the same expression is that it is a play on 'cacked' from 'cack' meaning 'excrement', but there is no evidence to show that kind of progression.

## cattle dog

I stood by the waggon of Curran Deen the hawker and watched the herd of tired cattle passing by. Bearded drovers, sitting loosely on sweat-caked horses, flicked the lowing Herefords with long black whips, and blue cattle dogs trotted behind, panting, with their pink tongues almost on the ground.

Joe Wright, 'Indira' in *The Strength of Tradition*,
R. F. Holt ed., 1983.

The history of the Australian cattle dog, which was fully established in 1890, reads more like a paint chart than anything else. You begin with the blue-mottled smooth Scotch collie imported from Scotland by a squatter in the Hunter Valley, New South Wales. These dogs were described as 'merle', a word of uncertain origin meaning 'bluish-grey mottled with black'. Combine the Scottish merles with the dingo and you have a quiet, hardy dog of great use in working cattle, but without the instinct to protect property and apparently none too good with horses. So, take one dalmatian, mix and stir. The result—the merle blends with the spots to produce speckles, thus explaining the other names for the cattle dog, the Australian blue-speckle cattle dog or blue heeler. Red speckles or plain red are also possible.

## chalet

Join with Don and Kaye Mathews in their picturesque surroundings for self-contained or serviced accommodation, in fully equipped luxury one- and two-bedroom chalets famous for their mountain views.

*Mercury* (Hobart), 1989.

Dwelling places often give rise to uniquely local words not found in anyone else's English. In Australian English, for example, we have the 'home unit', a simple item that we might not suspect of being an Australianism. More particular still are words like 'govie' or 'guvvie', the abbreviation used by Canberra residents for a government-owned house. And then there are the terms for all the little extras either attached to the house or built on its grounds to make the accommodation go that little bit further. There is the 'sleep-out'—usually a roughly enclosed part of the verandah. And then there is the 'weekender' which in certain states and circumstances (mountainous terrain such as in the Dandenongs or in Tasmania) turns into the 'chalet', an A-frame building reminiscent of a Swiss chalet. The notion of a two-room chalet is mildly amusing. The 'granny flat' is not our own word but the use of 'bungalow' in Victoria for the self-contained flat in the bottom of the garden is a localism. The most curious of all of these is, I think, the 'badger box' which preserves the now obsolete reference to the wombat as a badger. The 'badger box' is an inverted V shelter, the name being an obsolete Tasmanian term which has nevertheless turned up as a contemporary name for a bush hut.

## chiack

> Hugh and Saul sat playing cards in the kitchen far into the night. Mollie wakened to hear them laughing, chiacking and black-guarding each other good-humouredly.
>
> Katharine Susannah Prichard, *Coonardoo: The Well in the Shadow*, 1929.

This is a golden oldie of Australian English—these days we would be more inclined to 'take the mickey'. Or rather the male half of the population would, because this fairly savage teasing regarded as a mark of great affection is essentially a guy thing. It seems, looking at a citation from the early 1900s, that chiacking was rather more serious and had violent intent. Just as boys practise swearing at each other to indicate their goodwill and esteem, so they indulge in chiacking with the result that the meaning of the word has softened from abuse to good-natured banter.

The origin is in British English—the costermonger's cry of commendation 'chi-ike'—turned ironic and aggressive. The earliest example of it is from a costermonger verse dated 1869:

'Now my pals I'm going to slope,
See you soon again I hope,
My young woman is awaiting, so be quick,
Now join in a chiyike, the 'jolly' we all like.'

(A jolly in this context is a cheer.)

## Christmas pudding

And speaking of plum pudding, I consider it one of the most barbarous institutions of the British. It is a childish, silly, savage superstition, it must have been a savage inspiration, looking at it all round—but then it isn't so long since the British were savages.

Henry Lawson, 'The Ghosts of Many Christmases' in
*The Romance of the Swag*, 1907.

Is it 'Christmas pudding' or 'plum pudding' to you? Colonial Australia seemed to tuck into its 'plum pudding' as did Victorian England, but since then we seem to have drifted towards 'Christmas pudding', perhaps out of disappointment at the lack of plums. Despite Henry Lawson's diatribe, the pudding stuck throughout the twentieth century, although of late saner voices have been promoting more digestible

Christmas fare. There haven't been plums in the pudding since the seventeenth century when domestic economies in Britain forced the substitution of raisins for the dried plums or prunes. Australians now seem to favour the emphasis on Christmas, however, and the references to 'plum pudding' are dwindling.

## chunder

This average Australian sees nothing wrong in Auntie Elizabeth gobbling a box of powders a day. As long as he doesn't swear or chunder on the carpet, Uncle Edwin can have his daily bottle of brandy, too.

Suzy Jarratt, *Permissive Australia*, 1970.

This peculiarly Australian term has been with us for roughly fifty years. There once was a popular notion that it was derived from the phrase 'watch under' used by seasick sailors on the upper decks as a warning to those below. But a nautical origin would mean that the word would have travelled the world rather than staying put in Australia. It is more likely that 'chunder' is a piece of good old Australian rhyming slang. The illustrator and cartoonist Norman Lindsay created a character known as 'Chunder Loo of Akim Foo', who appeared in the *Bulletin* in the 1910s and 1920s. 'Chunder Loo', of course, rhymes with 'spew'! And naturally, as with most rhyming slang, the rhyme word is dropped thus making the word intelligible only to those in the know.

## Clayton's

> Australia waited agog last week as our newest boy wonder Treasurer, Paul Keating, ascended the rostrum to deliver the Hawke Government's first excursion into the tried and true realm of Clayton's politics: the mini budget you have when you're not having a mini budget.
>
> *Sun-Herald* (Sydney), 22 May 1983.

Creating a brand new word is something that is quite difficult to do. The success story of the 1980s has to be 'Clayton's'—the thing you have when you don't have the thing. The advertising line—'It's the drink I have when I'm not having a drink'—was invented by Noel Delbridge, the creative director of D'Arcy, MacManus & Masius, and spoken by Jack Thompson for the soft drink Claytons Tonic.

In its early days the Clayton's reference was usually spelled out in full as in the quotation above. But by the end of the 1980s it was dropped in without explanation on the understanding that the audience would correctly interpret it. I have even found a citation for it in the *Straits Times* of Singapore, proving that it has travelled at least a little way beyond our shores and our English.

## cockatoo

Crown and anchor men were in every mess. Ours had a 'cockatoo' outside the door with one end of a piece of string in his hand and the other end tied to the operator's ankle. When an officer appeared, the 'cockatoo' tugged the string and in two seconds there was no sign of the game. One man would shove the board up his tunic, another pocket the crown and anchor pieces.

Patsy Adam-Smith, *The ANZACS*, 1978.

The cockatoo is a bird that tends to make its presence felt, so it is not surprising that it has woven itself into the language in various ways. The notion of the lookout as a kind of 'cockatoo', alert and wary as the bird, dates back to the early part of the eighteenth century. In any kind of illegal activity such a lookout was essential. More particularly, in two-up a 'cockatoo' is appointed to keep his eyes and ears open and warn the players of approaching representatives of the law.

It is thought that the word 'cockatoo' itself derives from the Portuguese 'cacatua'. The Portuguese picked up the name from the Malays, whose name for the bird, 'kakatuwa', was perhaps an attempt to echo the sound the birds made. It is also the Malay word for pincers with reference to the bird's beak.

[69]

## cocky farmer

A 'cocky' is a small farmer. He usually selects himself a three-hundred or five-hundred-acre holding, clears it, fences it, pays for it, sows wheat in it—and then he goes to bed to wait for his crop. The next morning he gets up and finds the paddock white with cockatoos grubbing up his seed. He is there to sow and reap— cockatoos. And that, they say, is how he got the name of a cockatoo farmer—a cocky.

C. E. W. Bean, *On the Wool Track*, 1910.

This is a nice explanation and no doubt one which held sway in the popular tradition of Bean's day. Other explanations along the same lines convey the idea that the squatters saw the small farmers as a scavenging horde and likened them to the cockatoo scratching for a living. Another possibility links the cockatoo farmer to Cockatoo Island in Sydney, which in the early days of settlement was a prison for intractable convicts. A settlement established at Port Fairy in Victoria in the 1840s relied on tenant farmers referred to as 'cockatoo settlers' from Sydney.

'Cockatoo' was shortened to 'cocky' and used in other combinations—'cocky country' was land divided up into small holdings and 'cocky's delight' or 'cocky's joy' was golden syrup. It was also used in reverse combinations such as 'cow cocky' and 'cane cocky'.

## cooee

> There was also a moment when Hugh, out in front, in the middle of a bridge, took it into his curly head to stop, put some of his gear on the sleeper he stood on, and let out an Australian 'Cooee'. He said he wanted to test the gorge for echoes.
>
> Harold Lewis, *Crow on a Barbed Wire Fence*, 1973.

This was originally a call used by the Aborigines, specifically noted in the early days of contact between the Dharug and the white colonists. It was described as a penetrating clear call, with the first syllable prolonged and then jerked sharply upwards at the end. The various spellings—'co-wee', 'cooey'—have been attempts to capture the sound. To be 'within cooee' is to be 'within hearing range', although this phrase is used more often figuratively than literally. The 'cooee' was a popular symbol of the Australian way of life in colonial times, and songs and poems were written which took advantage of its musical potential. In the recruiting marches for World War I, the 'cooee' calling our boys to war had symbolic overtones and led to 'The Cooee March', a recruiting drive that went from rural New South Wales through the city of Sydney. These days 'cooee' seems to suffer from colonial quaintness, although every Australian child, I am sure, still learns it as part of that vestigial bushmanship that city kids love to think they are mastering.

## coolgardie safe

> Once, one hot day at Sandalwood, he and his cousin Didi had got into the big Coolgardie safe on the back veranda and closed the door. It was very cool in there, water seeping continually down the clinker-packed walls. They shared the safe with half a sheep, and amused themselves by swinging the meat back and forth on its hook like a punching-bag.
>
> Randolph Stow, *The Merry-Go-Round in the Sea*, 1965.

The 'coolgardie safe' is an ingenious Australian device which works on the principle that water loses heat when it evaporates. The 'safe' is a framework usually covered with hessian which dips into a water container. As the water seeps along the fine fibres of hessian it evaporates and this process draws heat out of the safe and causes a drop in the temperature of the safe and its contents.

The inventor is said to be A. P. McCormick and the invention is dated to the goldrushes of the 1890s in Western Australia. McCormick went on to become the mayor of Coolgardie, a career path which demonstrates the public-spirited thinking of a man who named his invention not after himself but after his town.

Another ingenious device of the outback which works on the same principle is the canvas waterbag. The rush of air created by a moving vehicle passes over the waterbag strung from its side, causing evaporation and producing cool drinking water at the end of the journey.

## coolibah

Towards evening we once again began to look for a pleasant camping-site. We found it by a lily lagoon fluttering with bird life. Rimmed by shady coolibahs, the lagoon was a scoop of gleaming water a hundred yards wide and a quarter of a mile long.

Coralie and Leslie Rees, *Spinifex Walkabout*, 1953.

The coolibah tree that the swagman camped under in 'Waltzing Matilda' could have been one of a number of eucalypts of inland Australia. Coolibahs grow on the banks of rivers or creeks or waterholes where occasional rains raise the level of water. In particular, the 'coolibah' is taken to be *Eucalyptus microtheca*, a tree that grows to twelve metres, with long, narrow, bluish-grey leaves. This was the tree upon which Burke and Wills read the 'Dig' message. 'Coolibah', sometimes spelled 'coolabah', is an anglicisation of the Aboriginal word 'gulabaa' from the Yuwaalarraay language spoken in northern New South Wales.

## corroboree

Our life was a tribal life, though some of the natives in the pocket would roam outside it, and go to distant places on trading marches or to attend some big corroboree that demanded their presence.

W. E. Harney, *Brimming Billabongs*, 1947.

## corroboree

This word was borrowed from the Dharug language spoken near Sydney and probably referred to a style of dancing. The elements of a 'corroboree' are singing and dancing, and the acting out of stories taken either from tradition or from contemporary events. A 'fighting corroboree' was one organised to settle a grievance between two groups in a ritualised way. One of the early mentions of the 'corroboree' (1825) notes the distinctive way in which the music starts high, and then falls away until it reaches the lower octave, upon which it returns to the high pitch. In modern musicology, this has been termed the 'tumbling strain'.

In colonial Australia the 'corroboree' was also used to name the festivities of the white settlers, but usually with a feeling that this was in jest and with a strong consciousness of the allusion to the real 'corroboree'. In more poetic vein the settlers might have remarked on a 'corroboree of birds'. Both these uses were essentially colonial.

## cove

'Well, if that ain't the cheekiest thing I ever heard tell of,' says I laughingly. 'To put up a yard at the back of a man's run, and muster his cattle for him!…But suppose the cove or his men come across it?'

Rolf Boldrewood, *Robbery under Arms*, 1889.

James Hardy Vaux is one of the earliest sources of information about Australian English. His qualifications for the task of lexicographer include three separate transportations to New South Wales for forgery, and an unusual degree of language awareness in his time as a convict. Vaux was prompted by his own observations of the gap between the dialects of English spoken in the context of court by the judges and by the convicts, and took it upon himself to act as translator. His *Flash Language*, written in 1812, was meant to be a guide to the uninitiated in the meaning of convict argot. One item which occurs in this vocabulary is 'cove'. Vaux says: 'the master of a house or shop is called the Cove; on other occasions, when joined to particular words, as a cross-cove, a flash-cove, a leary-cove, etc., it simply implies a man of these several descriptions; sometimes, in speaking of any third person, whose name you are either ignorant of, or don't wish to mention, the word cove is adopted by way of emphasis.'

All these uses are evident in Australian English: 'flash cove', 'leary cove' and 'cross cove' turn up in colonial texts along with 'bush cove'. But one use of 'cove' which had particular significance in colonial life was the one that is illustrated above, 'the cove' as the manager of a property, equivalent to 'the Boss' or 'the Man'.

## creek

A creek is commonly the bed of a stream, which being partially exhausted during the dry weather, forms only an occasional pond or water-hole.

W. H. Breton, *Excursions*, 1833.

This is one of those words which we would expect to be understood the world over, given its frequency and its 'ordinariness' in the context of Australian English. The Americans would understand us because we share a colonial history and the word has taken the same path in both Englishes, but the British would be surprised. As far as they are concerned a 'creek' is 'a narrow inlet on the coastline', or 'an inlet or short arm of a river'.

The origin of the word is lost in Germanic mists of time and lack of lexicography, but the starting-off point in a range of related languages seems to be this fundamental notion of 'a small indent in the coastline'. Sometimes the word seems to link with 'crack', sometimes with 'crook'.

The first citation for 'creek' in Australian English comes from the journal of John Hunter in 1793 where he uses 'creek' in the English sense of 'the coastal inlet'. From there on the more important sense seems to be 'the short arm of a river'. The emphasis shifts from the notion of 'a little corner or crook of the river' to the idea that this water flow is a subsidiary of the main branch which in its turn feeds into a river, lake or ocean. What the scale of the flow is and indeed whether it is there at all becomes increasingly irrelevant. The 'creek' can be as big as a river, or it can be a dry and dusty bed which only fills with water after heavy rain.

## crook

'What's happened to me, dearie?' she questioned in a wheezy whisper.

'You fell downstairs last night and hurt yourself pretty badly. How do you feel this morning?'

'I feel crook. Something's happened to me leg.'

Norman Lindsay, *Dust or Polish?*, 1950.

'Crook' is a very expressive word in Australian English. It can mean sick, as in 'I feel crook', or angry, as in 'Don't go crook (or crooked) on me', or shonky, as in 'That was a crook deal'. All these meanings go back to one of those fundamental distinctions—something can be straight or it can be twisted. Metaphorically speaking, something straight is good, fine, pleasing and honest, while something twisted is bad, disturbing, distressing and dishonest. Buried in British dialectal use, this idea has become mainstream in our English. This figurative use is paralleled by the thieves' use of the expressions 'on the cross' (dishonest) and 'on the square' (honest). In later colloquialism if you were 'tracking square' with a girl, then you were honest in your intentions towards her.

## cultural cringe

This sense of inadequacy in relation to England contoured the outlook of the Australian elite in endless ways: it gave rise to what A. A. Phillips has called the 'cultural cringe', to much of what Rose describes as 'the derivative element' in our culture, which we can probably run to earth in an undefined desire to be more English than the English, more genteel than the genteel.

Miriam Dixson, *The Real Matilda*, 1984.

We cringe in fear, but more specifically in situations where we wish to show that we are lowly and unworthy beings deferring to a superior. A culture cringes when it deems itself to be forever and in all situations inferior to another culture. Initially, the Australian cultural cringe deferred to all things British, but there are examples of it in relation to America as well.

The term was coined in 1950 by the literary critic A. A. Phillips, who was commenting on the oppressive weight of Anglo-Saxon culture which bears down on the Australian writer and inhibits their freedom of expression. Christopher Wallace-Crabbe refers to the difficulty the writer has in achieving a convincing naturalness with the 'European ghosts that lean over one's shoulder and jog one's pen'. From this literary context the term has broadened to cover all aspects of Australian life.

## currency lad

Now Hume was a currency lad, and Hovell belonged to
the sterling, those men who believed that the accident
of place and station of birth had conferred on them a
superiority of character and talent over the currency
lads and lasses. So an expedition designed to increase
man's knowledge of a harsh and elemental land developed into a trial of strength between a currency lad and
a bloody immigrant.

Manning Clark, *A History of Australia*, 1968.

This expression comes from the experiences of the new colony
in managing a local money system known as 'colonial
currency' which was discounted against British sterling. For
most of the first fifty years of settlement there was an obvious
distinction between 'currency' and 'sterling', which became a
symbol of a broader antagonism of the locals or native-born
to the British blow-ins. Colonial currency was always of less
value than sterling. Whatever hopes and aspirations a currency
lad had, they would be dashed against the unassailable superiority of the British.

# (Dd)

### daggy

> When I told kids at school I'd be marching for Legacy,
> they all killed themselves laughing. 'Talk about daggy',
> one of them muttered. I desperately wanted to be like
> them, but I just didn't seem to be made of the right
> stuff.
>
> Sally Morgan, *My Place*, 1987.

It is in this pejorative sense that 'daggy' survives in Australian
English. The daggy person is the odd and eccentric character,
and being odd, particularly in the context of adolescence, is
not a good thing. In the dialect of Somerset a dag was a boy's
term for 'a daring feat', and the game was to match dag for
dag. The person who did the best and most spectacular dags
was the object of admiration.

The other kind of 'dag' is from northern British dialects

and refers to a lock of wool on a sheep which is stiff with excrement. A daggy sheep has not had its daglocks removed. In this sense applied to a person 'daggy' was the equivalent of 'scungy', but this usage is dying out.


## damper

Then the fire I start and the water I get,
And the corned beef and damper in order I set,
But I don't touch the grub, though so hungry I be,
I will wait till it's ready—the Billy of Tea.
Anon, 'Billy of Tea' in *Native Companion Songster*, 1889.

---

Colonial life in Australia was sustained on tea and meat accompanied by damper, unleavened bread cooked over the ashes of the fire. The art and craft of lighting, sustaining and relighting fires was common knowledge in the bush and indeed in the towns before the electrical revolution. A good campfire needed to be economical (that is, not burn too much wood), burn slowly providing good heat, and still be alive under the ashes when you wanted it quickly in the morning. The fire was at some point covered with ash to keep the coals burning slowly and this practice was called 'damping the fire'. It has been suggested that wet dough had much the same effect and that the blanket of dough acted as a damper. Or perhaps it was that the appetites of the bushmen were 'damped' by bread of such consistency.

[81]

## deadset

> Here yar. Have me lunch. Deadset, I'm not hungry, I
> just had a curried chop in Home Science...
> Gabrielle Carey and Kathy Lette, *Puberty Blues*, 1979.

'Dead' as a colloquialism meaning 'completely' has a long
record in British English. The notion that someone looks as
if they are dead lies behind such a phrase as 'dead drunk'.
From this we make the transfer to the meaning 'completely'
which then gives rise to another set of constructions, such as
'dead broke' .

To be 'set' is to be decided. You can be either 'set on'
something (in favour of it) or 'set against' something (opposed
to it). To be 'deadset' is to take an extreme and resolute point
of view. This particular collocation seems to have made more
of a mark in Australian English than in any other variety. We
have the expression of surprise 'Dead set!', the adjective as in
'deadset winner', and the adverb as in 'He deadset did!'

## didgeridoo

> In unison they stamped and lunged, telling the tale of
> their adventures, each in turn, in a rapid high-pitched
> sentence snatched from each other's lips—A black bull
> charged me—he was a monster—a great black devil—
> he killed my horse—the blood of my horse—swept over

me reeking—I flew at the devil—mad with rage—
because he killed my brother the horse—and grasped
his horns—and flung him to the earth—and in a storm
of dust and blood—broke his neck—accompanied by
the compelling staccato click of the music-sticks and the
reverberating bellow of the great pipes called didjeri-
doo and the intermittent rising and falling chanting of
the squatting crowd.

Xavier Herbert, *Capricornia*, 1938.

The name of the 'didgeridoo' is from the Yolngu language,
one of a group of closely related languages from north-eastern
Arnhem Land. In the Aboriginal language the name was
imitative of the sound made by the instrument, as noted by
one writer for *Smith's Weekly* in 1919, who commented that it
had but one sound—'didgery, didgery, didgery'. As is usual
with such borrowings, the first impulse of the settlers was to
capture the sound in an anglicised form and this resulted in
the standard spelling 'diridgery doo'. Lately, 'didjeridu' has
resurfaced, a spelling which gives greater recognition to its
Aboriginal origin. The mark of its anglicisation is the shortened form 'didge'.

## digger

Money was loose, and the diggers, if given long credit
when down on their luck, were in the main to be relied

on to pay up when they struck the lead or tapped a
pocket.

Henry Handel Richardson, *The Fortunes of Richard
Mahony*, 1917.

The Californian gold mines established the use of 'diggings'
and 'digger' in a specific mining context. That use transferred
to the Australian goldfields with the influx of American
miners. The ethic of the digger was one of mateship, because,
just as bush life had been dangerous for the lone settler,
mining was practically impossible for one man to do alone.
Prospectors may have been solitary but diggers worked
together.

During World War I 'digger' acquired a new connotation
and referred to the infantryman who was at the front line and
forever digging in the trenches. Australian prime minister
Billy Hughes was affectionately nicknamed the 'Little Digger'
by Australian troops he visited in France.


**dillybag**

Jamie put down the paper and saw the dillybag in the
dead hands. The ancient Aboriginal dillybag the
Professor had once shown him. Made by gins long dead
from possum skin and human hair and embroidered in
coloured seeds.

Ronald McKie, *The Mango Tree*, 1975.

Versions of the Aboriginal dillybag have been manufactured as useful or decorative small carrybags. The original was made from grass or fur twisted into a cord which was then woven into a string bag used by women. 'Dilly' does in fact mean 'bag', but the European settlers doubled up, making it into 'dillybag'. The word comes from the language of the Yagara, who lived in the Moreton Bay district in south-eastern Queensland. It was the name for a particular kind of coarse grass from which the bags were woven, but by association came to refer to the bag itself. The 'grass' appears to be fronds from the Xanthorrhoea or grass tree which are extremely tough. 'Dilly' is a word that made the transfer into Australian English in the early days of white settlement in Moreton Bay, so the first examples of it date back to the early 1800s.

## dingo

I wasn't used to the weird noises made by the wild animals: the sharp, piercing howl of the wild dog or dingo. The dingoes were close to me and no doubt watching me all night. One of them would howl and then a few minutes later its mates would answer. Each time one howled close to me, a funny, frightened feeling went up and down my spine.

Albert Facey, *A Fortunate Life*, 1981.

The 'dingo' was the domesticated dog of the Aborigines, whereas the 'warrigal' was the same dog in the wild. Both words are from the Dharug language. Both words developed a range of meanings in Australian English.

The dingo acquired a bad reputation with settlers, who accused it of killing sheep and felt that, even when it appeared to be tame, it did not have the same respect for livestock that their own dogs had. So a 'dingo' as a person, a 'human dingo', was someone thought to be cowardly and treacherous.


**dob**

He knew I'd been initiated, but so had he too when he was a kid, and he knew that yuh don' dob no one in— or else…

William Dick, *A Bunch of Ratbags*, 1965.

In British dialect 'to dob someone' is 'to knock them over' or 'put them down'. It is a variant of 'dab', both words having somewhat heavier implications than we would anticipate. In Yorkshire dialect circa 1870 if you 'dabbed someone's nose', blood would undoubtedly begin to flow. From this rough physicality we leap to a figurative knockout—the person you 'dob in' has been given a metaphorical king hit. There is broad speculation that our aversion to 'dobbers' springs from our convict past and the belief that however unappealing the activities of others might be, you stuck by your class and never turned 'one of us' over to 'one of them'. It is interesting, however, that evidence for the word 'dobbing' is found from the mid-1950s, comparatively late.

## donga

> While everyone else was out in the donga learning to disguise themselves as anthills and sneak up on the enemy, I was in the kitchen heading a crack team of cleaners composed of no-hopers like Peebles.
>
> Clive James, *Unreliable Memoirs*, 1980.

This word is borrowed from South African English, probably at the time of the Boer War. It comes from Xhosa and Zulu *udonga* meaning 'a gully or watercourse'. These watercourses were formed by water erosion but were mostly dry, thus giving cover to soldiers. In Australian English 'donga' had this general meaning but also came to refer to a phenomenon of desert country—a round depression that held water from times of heavy rain so that the growth within it was lush compared with its surrounds.

'Donga' then came to mean any rough shelter, probably as a transfer from the war experience of the sheltering gullies in South Africa. The donga experience has stretched as far as Antarctica where originally it referred to a hut but has since become generalised to mean sleeping quarters even if they are located in a more permanent building.

## donkey vote

The donkey-votes mostly affect elections for the Senate.

George Mikes, *Boomerang: Australia Rediscovered*, 1968.

Australian politics has added few items to our vocabulary. It may not be something to boast about but we are responsible for the term 'donkey vote' which refers to the collective vote of those citizens who, while compelled to vote, are not compelled to give any thought to their preference and so mark their voting paper starting from the top and ending at the bottom. This puts the position on the page above any actual decision-making or selection of preferred candidates. The 'donkey vote' can be counted on only in countries which have compulsory voting but where that happens, the pundits will make use of this political Australianism. It makes you proud!

## Dorothy Dixer

Labor came up with a simple but effective method today of curtailing the drone of Education Minister David Kemp. As Dr Kemp waffled on in response to

a Dorothy Dixer, the Opposition benches erupted
with chants of 'boring', 'boring'.

AAP News Service, 9 March 1999.

A 'Dorothy Dixer' is a pre-arranged question asked in parliament of a minister by a member of the government, specifically to pave the way for a propagandist reply. The term for it was presumably dreamed up as a sneer by an opposition party—although there is no evidence to show who coined the term—since it refers to the pen-name, Dorothy Dix, of US journalist Elizabeth Meriwether Gilmer (1870–1951). Her advice column was thought to be partly based on letters created by Gilmer herself. Reference to the parliamentary practice first appears in the early 1960s. It's hard to imagine an agony aunt making such a deep impression, especially one who worked for a New Orleans paper called the *Daily Picayune*. Yet 'Dorothy Dix Talks', written between 1896 and 1901, made her famous and led to fifty years of advice syndicated in newspapers around the world.

## Down Under

The Pacific war, in one commentator's words, meant
that, 'No longer was Australia an imperial Antipodes,
but the New Frontier down under'.

Joan Beaumont, *Australia's War 1939–45*, 1996.

There are several terms for Australia or parts of the country that appear to have an image of the world as a globe in mind. The Antipodes, meaning Australia, is so named because it is viewed as being on the opposite end of the earth's surface to Britain. This gave rise to the related term 'Down Under' which first appeared in the 1880s.

Within Australia we have the Top End, which usually refers to the northern part of the Northern Territory, but sometimes more generally to the coastal areas of the north. The city of Palmerston which became Darwin was established in 1869. The use of Top End and Top Ender became general in the early 1900s.

## Dreaming, the

> They did not know yet that the 'dreaming' was over for the Boontamurra and soon enough for all the wandering ancient tribes of the whiteman's big new colony.
> Mary Durack, *Kings in Grass Castles*, 1959.

The translation of the Arrernte word 'alcheringa', sometimes 'alchuringa', that was popular in the 1890s was 'dreamtime' but later analysis of 'alcheringa' into 'altyerre' meaning 'dream' and '-nge' meaning 'from' or 'of' made that translation seem too limited. 'Alcheringa' was not just the long ago but the here and now as well. The notion of a 'dreamtime' seemed to locate it solely in the past. From the 1940s 'dreaming' comes into play, at least as an alternative to 'dreamtime', with the sense that one can encounter 'dreamings' in the physical world now, places that are linked in Aboriginal tradition and spirituality with the creation period. Stories of the Dreaming are explanations of the physical world, of how particular landmarks appeared, how rivers and seas were created, and of how human beings appeared on the earth.

## drongo

The trouble with Superman, Captain Marvel, Captain Marvel Jr, Batman and the rest of the dual-identity squad was that no one thought much of them when they were in mufti. Lois Lane practically wore her lip out sneering at Clark Kent while the poor drongo stood there and took it.

Clive James, *Unreliable Memoirs*, 1980.

Poor Drongo will be forever remembered as the horse that never won a race and whose name was adopted as a perennial insult. It is a trifle unfair as the horseracing records of the 1920s show that, while he never won, he was not always last. He performed quite well, coming second, third, fifth, etc., and should be regarded as unlucky rather than as a complete no-hoper. Exasperated punters appear to have turned on the unfortunate Drongo, however, and Australian English has gained another localism for a complete idiot.

## drover

> With the bullock muster it was speed and moving all the time, as the young and old bullocks were rounded up to be handed over to some waiting drover, who would drive them to the holdings farther in, where they would be fattened for the city markets.
>
> W. E. Harney, *Brimming Billabongs*, 1947.

This word has a long but minor history in British English. In Old English a 'drove' was a group of animals driven somewhere. From a drove of horses the leap was made to a drove of people, from which we get the expression 'to come in droves'. The drover was the person who herded the animals, often along a section of unenclosed road in a common, known as a 'drove road'.

For us, though, the term 'drover' conjures up Australian bush life where the drovers took tracks that crossed the length and breadth of the country. The drover was synonymous with the bushman as a stereotype of endurance and survival skills.

An earlier name for the drover was 'overlander', a term which originally referred to the cattle route overland from New South Wales to Adelaide. And then there was the drover's dog, ever faithful and hardworking. Over time this dog came to be seen as a drudge, doing the same old rounds day after day, which explains Bill Hayden's famous remark in 1983—that a drover's dog could have led the Labor Party to victory.

## dude

Mary Wall was twenty-five. She was an Australian bush girl every inch of her five-foot-nine…She said she was going to be an old maid. There came a jackeroo on a visit to the station. He was related to the bank with which Wall had relations. He was a dude, with an expensive education and no brains. He was very vain of his education and prospects. He regarded Mary with undisguised admiration, and her father had secret hopes.

Henry Lawson, 'The Bush-Fire' in
*The Romance of the Swag*, 1907.

'Dude' is, as we all know, an American word. It originally referred to a refined or pretentious man who was more concerned with grooming and effete manners than with being macho. Later on it came to mean any male person in general—equivalent to the Australian 'bloke'. Then, as with the word 'guy', teenagers starting using 'dude' to refer to both sexes. People may think that this is a recent borrowing and sadly reflects the Americanisation of our culture, but the word has been in Australia for many a year and, as well as Henry Lawson, it was used by Henry Handel Richardson and Ion L. Idriess. Despite this history, however, it has to be said that the current teenage use is largely due to American TV shows. Today the word doesn't simply mean 'a person' but rather 'a cool person'. A 'dude' is the antithesis of a dag, nerd, gumby, wuss, etc.

## dunny

> The municipal dunny cart was full up to the brim,
> The municipal dunny man fell in and couldn't swim,
> They saw the bubbles rising as he sank into the foam,
> And they heard the maggots crying,
> 'There's no place like home.'
>
> Wendy Lowenstein, *Improper Play Rhymes*, 1988.

This word is a shortening of the earlier 'dunnekin' which occurs in many British dialects. The origin of 'dunnekin' is uncertain but the best guess is that '-ken' means 'house' and 'dunne-' is related to the word 'dung'. This means that 'dunny' is literally equivalent to that other well-known Australian term, 'shithouse'.

In British dialect 'dunny' retained its basic meaning, 'an outside privy', but in Australian English it broadened its use to idioms such as 'lonely as a country dunny'. Its crowning glory was of course the imprecation, 'I hope your chooks turn into emus and kick your dunny down.'

# (Ee)

## echidna

> The spiny anteaters, known in the school books as echidnas and colloquially as porcupines, were great favourites. They are endearing in their helplessness and beauty with no protection but to burrow out of sight or to roll in a ball.
>
> Miles Franklin, *Childhood at Brindabella*, 1963.

There have been many names ascribed to the 'echidna'. For a while it was called the 'Australian hedgehog', but that seems to have been a colonial name which faded in the early 1900s. In the bush the echidna is still referred to as a 'porcupine'. It was commonly called the 'anteater' or 'spiny anteater', an apt name because it does indeed have a diet of ants. But 'anteater' seems to be going out of fashion, as if in some way it is thought to be incorrect or—even worse—American. Its common name today is what was once its zoological generic name, 'Echidna', ascribed to the animal by the French naturalist Cuvier in 1798 and derived from a Greek word meaning 'viper' with allusion to the long snake-like tongue. This classification was not ultimately accepted, being supplanted by the genus name 'Tachyglossus' (meaning 'swift tongue'), coined in 1811.

## esky

A small Esky with some chops and sausages in it might be standing in the shade of a banksia tree and when we'd had enough of the sea we might light a small fire. I could smell those chops now, feel that sun, hear those waves.

Neilma Sidney, 'The Fountain of Tbilisi' in
*Sunday Evening*, 1988.

This word is a classic example of a trademark that has gained popular currency in the language. Similar words, some of which many people no longer recognise as being originally trademark terms, include 'alfoil', 'araldite', 'bandaid', 'biro', 'bowser', 'cellophane' and 'doona', just to name a few.

The esky was originally released onto the market by Malleys Ltd in the 1950s. This early version was the sturdy metal type, with a drainage hole near the base. It was a huge success. The name was coined by shortening the word 'eskimo', with the ending assimilated to the common colloquial noun suffix '-y' or '-ie'. Later on other models were made of various materials—like styrofoam—which were lighter and much easier to carry. The esky has become ubiquitous at the Australian picnic and barbecue, and although other names have come along, such as 'chillybin', they have not displaced the original. In surfer talk, 'esky lid' is a derogatory term for a bodyboard or boogie board, connoting the family picnic at the beach. 'Esky lidders' are amateurs and do not belong in the world of serious surfing.

## eucalypt

He fled fifty yards into the open. Ending under a smooth and tolerant eucalypt and jumping to snatch down some of the leaves from its high branches, he crushed them in his hands and sniffed up their clean astringency. They stung his brain, and he dropped the ones he held and jumped for more.

Thomas Keneally, *Bring Larks and Heroes*, 1967.

The 'eucalypt', described by early European settlers as a drab and unlovely tree, but viewed now as a national emblem of Australia's natural beauty, had its name conferred on it by French botanist Charles Louis L'Héritier, friend to Joseph

Banks. L'Héritier published a book in London in 1788 in which he described examples of the eucalypt gathered from Adventure Bay in Tasmania by Cook on his third voyage. The particular tree that L'Héritier had in his hands was the *Eucalyptus obliqua*, now known as the 'messmate'. He noticed the peculiar shape of the buds which formed in a cup-shaped swelling with what seemed like a lid or cap snugly fitted. He thought the buds well-covered, so he reached, as botanists did in those days, into his knowledge of Greek and pulled out the words 'eu' meaning 'well' and 'calyptos' meaning 'covered'.

## Eureka

At ten on the morning of 30 November Commissioner Rede, supported by a troop of mounted and foot police, their swords drawn and their bayonets fixed, declared to the diggers that he was determined to inspect their licences. Some diggers shouted 'We haven't got them', some 'We have burnt them', some 'We will not have drawn swords and fixed bayonets', some 'Where is the governor?' and some 'We want justice and we will have it'…The diggers fell into line two abreast behind Captain Ross from Toronto who had hauled down the Southern Cross flag from yesterday's diggers' platform and bore it proudly for the march to Eureka, during which the diggers chanted slogans against paying the

licence fees and in favour of winning their rights.
Manning Clark, *A History of Australia*, 1968.

The 1850s were heady goldrush days in Victoria. The Eureka gold diggings, near Ballarat, were named from the story of how Archimedes worked out in his bath that a body would displace its own weight in water. 'Eureka' means 'I have found it'. Having shouted 'Eureka!', Archimedes left his bath to carry on with his experiments.

The dispute between the miners and Lieutenant Governor La Trobe about mining licences led some disgruntled diggers to refuse to pay. Led by Peter Lalor, they set up a stockade at Eureka and barricaded themselves against La Trobe's police. The story, as told by Raffaello Carboni in *The Eureka Stockade* published in 1855, turned a squabble over taxes into a fight of the people against the British government. It was also the beginnings of republicanism. The flag that was raised, known as the 'Eureka flag' or the 'Southern Cross', is similarly linked with the republican movement.

# (Ff)

**fair dinkum**

> Every sinful calico-jimmy roaming at large is an insult
> to the doctrine of 'fair dinkum' which all men, rogues
> or otherwise, hold in respect.
>
> *Bulletin*, 10 August 1895.

(A 'calico jimmy' was a member of the free-trade group who
lobbied for the importation of duty-free textiles at the end of
the nineteenth century.)

There is folklore in language as in everything else and one
of the most abiding popular beliefs about the phrase 'fair
dinkum' is that 'dinkum' is Chinese in origin and means 'true
gold'. It conjures up a vision of excited Chinese on the
goldfields, waving lumps of gold and shouting 'Dinkum!
Dinkum!', probably to distinguish their offering from the
buckets of fool's gold available. Alas, it is not true.

'Dinkum' is a word brought to Australia in the dialectal speech of the white settlers. It refers to a share of work requiring to be done, and then to work generally. In *Robbery under Arms* Boldrewood writes, 'It took us an hour's hard dinkum to get near the peak.' 'Fair dinkum' has in it the notion that the allotment of work should be moderate and just.

## fang

I had a Triumph Tiger 100 with a sidecar and we'd stack it up with surfos and Boof Bennett or Peter Troy would lie on top of them and we'd fang off along the cliffs on the old coach road.

*Age* (Melbourne), 21 February 1981.

One meaning of 'fang', which is home-grown in Australia, is to drive a vehicle at high speed. Young lairs and larrikins who have nothing better to do will just 'fang around' in their cars, doing wheelies, screechies, and hopefully charming members of the opposite sex. When they 'fang' it up the street, they put the pedal to the metal and really burn rubber.

This use of the word comes from the name of the famous Argentinian racing car driver Juan Fangio, whom all these young heroes attempt to emulate, and seems to date back to the 1960s. Fangio's racing career stretched from 1934 to 1958 during which he was world champion five times.

## farnarkeling

The Australian farnarkelers were literally on top of the world last night following their epoch-making victory against the formidable East German farnarkeling machine in a closely-contested final at the People's Farnarkeling Centre in light drizzle and heavy security in Moscow.

John Clarke, 'The Gillies Report', 1988.

This is a made-up word for a made-up activity and can therefore never claim a secure existence. Yet anyone who has ever been entertained by John Clarke is likely to know it. It is a word that he coined while writing and performing in the 1980s television series 'The Gillies Report'. 'Farnarkeling' is a fictitious team sport for which Clarke was the sports commentator. The rules and the jargon of the sport were therefore up to Clarke to invent. *The Macquarie Dictionary* also defines it as 'an activity which creates an appearance of productivity but which has no substance to it', while 'to farnarkel' or 'farnarkel around' is to engage in such activity.

Clarke, in an interview, said that he came up with 'farnarkeling' because there were different codes of football throughout Australia in winter and to choose any one of them would be limiting. It allowed him to focus on the true meaning of sport—the heroes, the triumphs, the defeats, the idolisation and the religious zeal—without being hampered by the facts of an actual sport.

[102]

**fossick**

> The sun had set, and weary walked
> The diggers from the mine;
> Well, a mine is not the name, although
> 'Twas in the digging line.
> 'Twas land where roving swagmen thought
> To fossick out some stuff;
> The gold, 'twas said, was near the top;
> Well, that was news enough.
>
> Bernard McElhill, 'A Bush Secret', c. 1880s.

'Fossick' is a word that sounds very much like what it is—a rummaging around, a searching here and there. It is a word from a British dialect that had its start in Australian English in the 1850s when goldminers fossicked through mullock heaps, turning over the dirt that others had tossed aside, in the hope that, if they searched diligently enough, they'd find that little bit of gold that the previous miner had missed.

In British dialect 'fossick' meant 'to find something out by asking around'. Lots of patient fossicking might turn up the information you wanted. To 'fussick' or 'fursick' was to potter over one's work, while to 'fussock' was to make a fuss or bustle about. The '-ock' or '-ick' ending implies repetitive action.

## furphy

'I don't believe it,' said Archy. 'I just don't bloody believe it. It's just another furphy.'

Jack Bennett, *Gallipoli*, 1981.

The firm J. Furphy & Sons Pty Ltd operated a foundry at Shepparton in the late 1800s. One of the items they made was a watercart. During World War I these watercarts were places where soldiers gathered, and inevitably at such gatherings they passed information around, often of dubious quality and amounting to no more than idle gossip. The name Furphy on the watercart became the word for the kind of false rumour that was generated around it.

# (Gg)

**galah**

> I tried to thank him for saving my life. He said he
> would have done the same for anybody, even a great
> useless, clumsy, splay-footed, mutton-headed galah of
> an Italian.
>
> Nino Culotta, *Gone Fishin'*, 1962.

The origin of 'galah' is straightforward enough—a borrowing
from the Yuwaalarraay language spoken near Lightning
Ridge in New South Wales. What is interesting is the
personality that we have given this bird. Why the galah
should seem to be more stupid than other birds is hard
to say. The connection between galahs and stupidity
seems to have asserted itself in the early 1900s and may
arise from the observation that, like cockatoos, galahs
like to chatter on. This notion occurs again in the name

given to the period on the outback radio network given over to private conversation. It was called the 'galah session'.

## gammon

> At last I got loose, and I walked on my way;
> A constable came up, and to me did say,
> 'Are you free?' Says I, 'Yes, to be sure, don't you know?'
> And I handed my card—'Mr William Barlow.'
> Oh dear, lackaday, oh;
> He said, 'That's all gammon' to Billy Barlow.
>
> Benjamin Griffin(?), 'Billy Barlow' in *Maitland Mercury and Hunter River General Advertiser*, 1843.

This word crossed from convict slang into the word store of the Aborigines, from there to a more widespread use in Aboriginal English as well as into general Australian English, particularly in the Top End where it is still used today.

Our earliest lexicographer, the convict James Hardy Vaux, records 'gammon' as meaning 'flatter, deceit, pretence, plausible language or any assertion which is not strictly true'. In a criminal context, the object of such patter is to deceive. Vaux goes on to explain: 'to gammon a person is to amuse him with false assurances…to obtain some particular end; to gammon a man to any act is to persuade him to it by artful language or pretence.' Vaux also writes of the word's more colloquial use, that is, 'to express astonishment and incredulity, usually of a good-natured sort accompanied with a smile and a shake of the head'.

Although the word can be traced in British English to the early 1800s, its history beyond that point is not clear. There is a speculative suggestion that behind it lies the image of the sellers of gammons of bacon in whose professional patter was the origin of the word. It is true that we do pick on particular stereotypes in the world of selling in this way—'spielers' in the circus world, used-car salesmen and so on, so it is possible that 'gammoners' were in their day the image of the sharp and manipulative persuaders.

## gibber

Everything looked big, felt big; all except the Camel-man who had a big job—gigantic! Towards the ever-receding horizon, far away across a gibber plain bearded with tufts of spinifex, he gazed unflinchingly.

Ion L. Idriess, *Flynn of the Inland*, 1932.

Dictionaries can do their best to help you to understand a word but sometimes there is no substitute for real-life experience. As I stood on my first gibber plain, I felt that the dictionary definition—'a smoothed and rounded weather-worn stone of the arid Australian centre'—had not really conveyed much to me. Now that I have seen the polished surfaces, the strange shapes, the different colours, and heard the rattle that gibbers make, one against the other, references to them in Australian writing make a great deal more sense.

The word 'gibber' is an Aboriginal borrowing, from the Dharug language, and the earliest reference to the word is dated 1790. It appears that the area now called The Rocks in Sydney was in the early 1800s referred to as 'the gibbers'. It is clear from these and other references that initially a 'gibber' was a rock of any size—from a small throwing stone to a large boulder. As 'a throwing stone' it equates to the 'brinnies' and 'yonnies' and 'goolies' of other districts and other Aboriginal languages. Today the word 'gibber' is narrowing in meaning to the kind of stone found on the plains of inland Australia.

### gidgee

Trees stretched out from the foot of the hills, acacia, thorn-bush and mulga; gidgee, round, dark-green and glossy-leafed, the water-tree, from whose roots, if you were bushed, you could get water.

Katharine Susannah Prichard, *Coonardoo:*
*The Well in the Shadow*, 1929.

'Gidgee' presents us with an identical anglicisation of two different words borrowed from two different Aboriginal languages. The 'gidgee' is a three-pronged spear, an item used by the Nyungar Aborigines of south-western Western Australia. It is also a species of acacia found in the dryer areas of inland Australia—this name is borrowed from the Wiradjuri tribe of central New South Wales. For both words there was a process of testing out various possible spellings; the spear was written 'gigie' or 'gidgee', and the bush as 'gidgea', 'gidyea', 'gidya', or 'gidgee'. The English spelling eventually settled for both on the same solution. As with all such homophones, context makes it clear which one is intended.

## gilgai

Landplaning gets the gilgais and other minor irregularities out of the ground.

*National Times*, 19 May 1979.

'Gilgais' are to be found in soils that contain a large amount of clay which swells and shrinks noticeably with wetting and drying. The result is a succession of bare depressions in what is otherwise a flat plain with scrubby vegetation—mulga or brigalow. The gilgai holes fill with water when it rains and dry out into hardened and cracked clay pans. They present a menace to horse and rider. They are sometimes referred to as 'crabholes' from the land crabs that inhabit them when they hold water.

**gilgai**

The word is from the Wiradjuri and Kamilaroi languages, spoken throughout a wide area from central to southern New South Wales. It is now a standard geographical term for this phenomenon wherever it occurs.

**goanna**

One day we say that we're a Christian nation and that we believe in salvation. The next thing we say 'preserve all the rituals and spirits of the goanna and the rest of it...' How do you find the spirit of the goanna?
Joh Bjelke-Petersen, *Johspeak*, 1988.

'Goanna' is not an Aboriginal borrowing as you might suspect but a variation of 'iguana'. The progression seems to be from 'iguana' to 'guana' (pronounced 'gew-anna') to 'gohanna' or 'goanna'. The shortening from 'iguana' to 'guana' happened in colonial American English and was transferred to other colonies as a general name for any large lizard. The further progression in colonial Australia was influenced by the pronunciation. The 'guana' spelling did not survive into the twentieth century where the 'goanna' spelling became the standard despite the fact that it no longer revealed its 'iguana' origin.

## gone to Gowings

If I say a person is too stupid to know 'whether it is Thursday or Anthony Horderns', or that, being astray as to wits she has 'gone to Gowings', my words only have meaning if my auditor understands that these are famous Sydney shops.

Nancy Keesing, *Lily on the Dustbin*, 1982.

The retail store Gowing Bros Ltd, still found in Sydney, came up with a very witty, and hence quite influential, advertising campaign in the 1940s. It ran a series of comic cartoons featuring someone who had just hastily departed, with the only explanation being that they had 'gone to Gowings'. One such ad shows a stunned wedding party looking at the bargain-hunter wife-to-be's note that she had 'gone to Gowings'.

One classic use was by the criminal Darcy Dugan. Apparently when he made one of his many famous escapes from jail he left a short note scrawled on the cell wall. It read: 'gone to Gowings'!

The expression picks up on the various meanings of 'gone', in particular 'gone in the head' or 'financially broke'. Context makes clear which sense is intended.

## Granny Smith

Or she would sit with Eve's fat white Persian cat in the packing shed, watching the apples tumble down the shute, and her mother, still with her long-ashed cigarette between her lips, lifting, swiftly wrapping in tissue, placing in arithmetic patterns the Granny Smiths, the Delicious, the perfect red Jonathons.

Jean Bedford, *Love Child*, 1986.

The 'Granny Smith' is still a popular apple partly because of its versatility as a cooking and eating apple, and because it keeps and travels well. It is named after Maria Ann Smith (c.1801–70) who grew the first apples of this kind in her orchard at Eastwood, then a rural area of Sydney, in the late 1860s. Her grandson says that she had received a shipment of a variety of crab apples (known as 'Tasmanian French Crabs') from an agent at the Sydney fruit markets to try out as cooking apples. Having cooked her apples she scattered the cores and peels on a flowerbed. The seedling that grew was the first of many apple trees to come.

## grouse

'How ya going?'
'Good. Real good.'
'Job okay?'

'Fine, fine—got a grouse pad, sharing with a coupla chicks and another guy.'

Mary Leslie, 'Bird in a Desert' in *A Bundle of Yarns*, Michael Kavanagh ed., 1986.

A recent collection of playground slang shows that 'grouse' is alive and well along with more modern indications of approval such as 'cool' and 'wicked'. This is an encouraging indication that our children aren't entirely overwhelmed by the language of American TV. Unfortunately, while clearly our own invention dating back to the 1920s, 'grouse' is of unknown origin. It is commonly used with an intensifier of some kind—'extra grouse' or even 'bloody grouse', never just mundanely 'grouse'.

## guy-a-whack

Fraudulent bookmakers of one kind and another are known as balancers, besters, crushers, snipers, knockers, guy-a-whack bookmakers, johnnycake bookmakers, blackmarketeers and bootleg bookmakers (the last four are virtually obsolete).

Sidney J. Baker, *The Australian Language*, 1966.

Even in the short history of Australian English we have some obsolete expressions. An odd example of this is 'guy-a-whack'. It is not evident why this word didn't succeed—'guy-a-whack' seems to have as much chance for glory as others like it, such as 'welsher', 'fly-by-night', 'absconder', 'decamper'.

The noun 'guy-a-whack' and its adjectival use shown in 'guy-a-whack bookmaker' both derive from the expression to 'guy a whack', which comes from the verb 'guy' meaning 'to decamp'. This in turn was a shorthand version of the phrases 'to do a guy' and 'to give the guy to'. The 'guy' in this instance is, according to the *Oxford English Dictionary*, Guy Fawkes— 'to do a guy' is to imitate the famous Guy and run off. Another suggestion is that it is rhyming slang, the rhyme being on 'Fawkes'. But in that case what is the rhyme?

The addition of 'a whack' seems to be one of those fairly meaningless but playful elaborations that are designed to refresh or beef up an expression that is getting a bit stale.

# (Hh)

## hambone

> Then the old lady of the bird having the turn said she'd ring the Johns so Sid chucked all over her and she got hysterical so Dennis belted her and then Phil did this king hambone on the kitchen table and ran round the house in the raw ripping the gear off all the birds—God he's KING!
>
> *Oz*, 1964.

The early history of this word is in the jargon of American theatre, where an impoverished actor of small talent had to use ham fat as the basis for stage makeup rather than more expensive, sweeter-smelling oils. Such people were known as 'hamfatters', and then as 'hams'. A hambone was a bad actor in a minstrel show (remember Mr Bones?) and dates back to the early twentieth century.

Lurking in all this, however, is the coarse colloquialism 'bone' for the penis. And so from this assorted theatrical collection, 1960s Sydney produced the hambone. The first evidence of its use cites medical students at Sydney University Orientation Week in 1964.

**hatter**

And yet most of us who were children in the eighties have some half-forgotten childish recollection of a tall gaunt figure in a long frayed overcoat, a shabby felt hat half hiding the sunken cheeks, a thin grey beard, and hard lines drawn as with a ruler across his face…With no other companions, he lived year in and year out— twenty, thirty, forty miles from the homestead…But seeing men so seldom, he came not to wish to see them—a 'hatter' they called him for his madness.

C. E. W. Bean, *On the Wool Track*, 1910.

The 'hatter' was the name given to the lonely prospector in the bush, and is mistakenly linked with the phrase 'as mad as a hatter'. That particular 'hatter' was mad because in the manufacturing of hats mercury was used in the felt, resulting in mercury poisoning. But the Australian 'hatter' was a man whose hat covered his family—a British colloquial expression of the 1800s which meant that he was all alone with no-one to look after but himself. The lonely prospector in the bush was remarkable in that most men worked in the bush in pairs—they were mates. Usually one of the results of the hatter's choice to go it alone was that he became 'ratty'—if not insane then at least eccentric.

## Hills hoist

*Rabbit on the Moon* is an amusing and touching story of Giuseppina, a cheeky Italian girl growing up in suburban Australia. While others have a Hills Hoist in the backyard, her family has a vegetable patch; while other kids eat peanut butter sandwiches, she munches on mortadella.

*Herald* (Melbourne), 1988.

Before the invention of the rotary clothes line, washing was hung on lines supported by two wooden poles with a movable arm so that one line was high as the other was lowered. As the supporting poles leaned in with the weight of the washing, the lines were propped up with wooden stays.

Lance Hill was to change the design of the suburban backyard. A motor mechanic in Adelaide, he found that the available space in his backyard was being encroached on by trees. Rather than cut back the trees, Hill decided to invent a space-saving hoist for drying the clothes. He came up with the idea in 1945 and put it on the market in 1946, and it has since become an icon of Australian life.

## hoon

> How much longer will the public in this State sit back and suffer the consequences of the actions of the scumbags and hoons who are slowly but surely tearing our society to shreds? Among other things, they're defacing our streets and our buildings and they're wrecking out suburban stations and our trains and buses.
>
> Letter to the editor, *Advertiser* (Adelaide), 1991.

The first meaning of 'hoon' that we have evidence for is that of 'pimp'. This is in Xavier Herbert's *Capricornia* published in 1938. It is clear from this insulting use that no male would have relished being called a 'hoon'. By the 1970s it was applied to any man who indulged in loutish behaviour of the kind associated with hoons in their role as standover men. Hoons were linked with barrackers of the early kind (see **barrack**). In the 1980s and 1990s the word drifted upmarket and came to mean much the same as 'lair'. To 'hoon around' has the same kind of carefree disregard of convention as 'lairise'.

### hooroo

'Hooroo, Charlie,' Betty called after him.
'Good-bye, Betty,' he answered without looking round,
and went out disconsolately.

Frank Hardy, *Legends from Benson's Valley*, 1963.

We have at our disposal a range of noises to say 'hello' and
'goodbye', and to express a range of emotions. Some of these
have a long history in which there are subtle changes both to the
form of the word and to the purposes to which it is put.
'Hooroo' with its variant form 'ooroo' seems to be linked to
'hurray'. When used as a farewell it has the stress on the first
syllable '*hoo*-ray'. Conversely as an expression of joy, in which
function it dates back to the 1700s in Britain, it has the stress on
the second syllable 'huh-*ray*'. 'Hooray' as a farewell seems to be
limited to rural Australia from north Queensland to Victoria.

An alternative theory is that it has its origin in a Dharawal
farewell for which 'Ooroo' or 'Uru' was a shortened version,
the longer one being used ceremonially and meaning literally
'May you travel well'. The Dharawal were a coastal people of
New South Wales whose travels extended as far as the southern side of Port Phillip Bay.

### humpy

Next morning when I woke up I found that the house
was a big mud brick humpy with a roof of corrugated

iron. There was no ceiling and no floorboards, just a dirt floor. The place had a lovely setting: in a flat, surrounded by huge granite hills.

Albert Facey, *A Fortunate Life*, 1981.

Aboriginal languages have given us a few names for makeshift shelters in the bush. One of these is the 'humpy' borrowed from the Yagara language spoken in the Moreton Bay district. In English this word can be applied to any dwelling that you think is cheap and nasty and falling down. 'Gunyah', borrowed in the early days of settlement from the Dharug tribe near Sydney, made a happier transfer into English where it came to be a romanticised word with pleasant and affectionate connotations. A reference to your gunyah would call up an image of a colonial cottage with verandah and chimney and the post-and-rail fence. But it is a word that has become obsolete today. 'Mia-mia' (from Aboriginal languages near Melbourne) and 'wurley' (from those near Adelaide) both refer to stacked up branches making a temporary shelter.

**hut**

In every thing Else it appears to be very Barren and the Natives sadly Distressd having only a few stragling low Hut & mostly Naked only with Ass cloaths...

William Noah, *A Voyage to Sydney in New South Wales in 1798–1799*, 1799.

The earliest use in British English of the word 'hut' seems to be a military one from the sixteenth century. The hut was the shelter of the soldier. It then came to mean any rough improvised dwelling, especially one seen as primitive. In this way it was applied to the gunyahs of the Aborigines. It also was used for the convict dwellings, and from this a basic social distinction in the colony arose. Huts belonged to convicts or assigned servants, but a 'house' was where the military officers and the gentry lived.

Even after the convict period ended and free men rather than assigned servants worked on the rural properties, they nevertheless continued to live in huts. The owner or station manager lived in a house. Just as the house had a housekeeper, some huts had a hut-keeper, who cleaned up the hut, did the cooking and so on. Station hands shared their hut with hut-mates. An improvised hut was a bush hut.

# (Ii)

## Illawarra shorthorn

Ours were shorthorns, big handsome creatures of various markings. Their hides ranged from pure white to dark red or a darker brindle, or spotted. The most handsome were the strawberry roans, 'a cattle carpet roan and red'.

Miles Franklin, *Childhood at Brindabella*, 1963.

The 'Illawarra shorthorn' has a long and respected history in Australia. The shorthorn was brought in the 1820s to the Illawarra district, that rich grazing country between Kiama and Nowra in New South Wales. It was a breed ideally suited for the colonial experience, and was similarly popular in America, being a medium-sized beast, red with white markings, somewhat angular and ungainly, but sturdy, reliable, and a good compromise between a milker and meat producer. It was crossed with the Devon and the Ayrshire and the new breed was established by the 1890s. In the twentieth century it was crossed with the Angus to produce the Murray grey, another Australian success story.

## illywhacker

Any person who uses a set routine of talk (a 'come-on') to secure victims is a 'spieler', 'eeler-spee', 'eeler-whack' and 'illywhacker' (the last three are formed by mutilation from the first: a trickster of this kind is said to 'whack the illy') .

Sidney J. Baker, *The Australian Language*, 1966.

'Illywhacker' is not a word that has had great frequency in Australian English and would probably have remained an obscure little item if Peter Carey had not resurrected it as the title of his novel. It is reminiscent of the way in which an odd little expression, 'waltzing matilda', was picked up and made a national icon by Banjo Paterson.

An 'illywhacker' is a small-time confidence trickster— but we really have so little evidence for the word that it is not clear what range of meaning it might have had. Kylie Tennant thought it meant a cheap crook 'selling imitation diamond pins, new-style patent razors or infallible "tonics"'. She also commented that the noun came from the phrase 'whack the illy'. Baker, on the other hand, suggests that the phrase follows the word, and that the word is a pig Latin distortion.

## imshi

> 'Exhibition,' he said. 'Very good, very nice, very clean, very syphilitic. Exhibisheeon can can. Exhibisheeon…' and the list followed. 'No,' said Pat. 'Imshi.'
>
> Lawson Glassop, *We Were the Rats*, 1944.

To 'imshi' is to exit at great speed, to skedaddle, to shoot through like a Bondi tram. It is a word borrowed from Arabic and acquired by the Australian Army in Egypt during World War I. By all accounts, soldiers picked up the local jargon quite fast. One man, who had only been in Egypt for a fortnight, recounted in his diary an incident in which he was obliged to protect his Arab guide 'who had got himself into an awful scrape' in the Sphinx temple. He told him to 'emshi yalla'—Arabic for 'Get out quickly'.

Military slang was brought back home where it mixed with civilian English. Like a number of words which have clearly been part of the lingo in the first half of the twentieth century, 'imshi' doesn't seem to be making the transfer into the more internationalised Australia of today. Two world wars meant that military jargon had some impact on Australian English in the twentieth century but it has much less influence today.

# (Jj)

**jabiru**

> The river swung north, south and west on a tortuous
> route through plain and range, cutting through dense
> pandanus thickets and tattered cadjibuts, cascading over
> rocky falls and into still reaches of pale blue lotus where
> jabiru and ibis preened and fished.
>
> Mary Durack, *Kings in Grass Castles*, 1959.

In his *Austral Dictionary* published in 1898, E. E. Morris listed
the 'jabiru' and stated that the word came from Brazil where
it was first applied to a large stork. His earliest citation for it
came from the explorer Ludwig Leichhardt, who commented
on his encounter with a 'Tabiroo'. The name comes from
Tupi-Guarani, an Indian language of Paraguay and Brazil.
The Australian stork was initially referred to as the 'New
Holland jabiru' to distinguish it from its South American

cousin. Both birds are large but the bird from Brazil is white with a red collar and black head. Our jabiru is also called the 'policeman bird', perhaps because of its glossy black and white uniform.

## jackaroo

> Of course not all gentleman jackaroos from Britain were weaklings and wastrels...When thirty shearers refused to commence work unless served with a free glass of grog a man, the Oxford jackaroo, 'with a few scientific taps delivered in the most gentlemanly manner', knocked out the ringleader, after which shearing proceeded smoothly.
>
> Russel Ward, *The Australian Legend*, 1966.

'Jack' was, in the last century, a common name for a man, and so 'Jack' came to be your average man—as in phrases like 'every man Jack of them' and 'jolly Jack Tar'. Picture your average 'Jack', put him beside a kangaroo to locate him unmistakably in Australia, and you have 'the jackaroo'. The only difficulty with this etymology is that the jackaroo was hardly the average man. He was usually English upper-class and aligned with the station owner rather than the working class, as the citation above indicates.

A less compelling claim, however, is that it comes from an

Aboriginal language where it is a name for the 'talkative cuckoo-shrike'.

## jarrah

> Just two kilometres down the main street...where a group of Nyungar families have made their home, is the gnarled old jarrah which marks the site of the Battle of Pinjarra. In days past a brass plate set into a recess cut in the trunk commemorated the battle. According to Oscar Little of Pinjarra, the plaque was stolen one night by white vandals who also attempted to burn down the jarrah.
>
> Al Grassby and Marji Hill, *Six Australian Battlefields*, 1988.

From the mid-1800s the 'jarrah' was commended as a wonderful timber—hard, durable, firm-grained. The name for the tree is from the Nyungar language spoken in the Perth–Albany region. Timbergetting was next to mining as a profitable nineteenth-century occupation for the Perth colonists, to the extent that an alternative to 'Sandgroperland' was 'Jarrahland' in popular parlance. The 'jarrah-jerker', though obviously originating in the timber industry, came to be a general term for anyone working in the bush.

## joey

> A young opussum (perhaps two or three days old) was
> put to a cat which had two kittens...It is really amusing
> to see the kittens crawling about with Joey clinging to
> one of their backs.
>
> *Trumpeter* (Hobart), 1828.

The first citation we have is with reference to the young of a possum. The creature is referred to as 'Joey' which may be one explanation—that in the absence of any official name in the lists of animals for the young of kangaroos, possums and echidnas, the diminutive pet name became the generic term. We think of a joey as the young of a kangaroo or wallaby, but it is a term applied to the young of possums, wombats and, surprisingly, cockatoos.

In colonial times it also applied to the young of domesticated animals—cattle and goats, which is interesting because 'calf' and 'kid' would have been the more obvious choice. And there has been the occasional slightly self-conscious reference to a human child. Ruby, a character in *The Shiralee*, comments when she has fainting fits that 'she was going to throw a joey at last'.

## johnny-cake

> The storekeeper measured me out a pannikin of dust
> into a newspaper and directed me to the left-hand

corner of the ram-paddock, as the best place for my horse. There, in the spacious Court of the Gentiles, I made a fire, worked up my johnny-cake on the flat top of the corner post, ate it hot off the coals, then lay down in swino-philosophic contentment, and read the newspaper till I could smell my hair scorching, and so to sleep.

Joseph Furphy, *Such Is Life*, 1903.

It seems clear that 'johnny-cake' is an Americanism dating back to the early 1700s meaning a cake of maize-meal toasted on a griddle. The etymology is not certain, though the word may well relate to the English dialect word 'jonnick' or 'jannock' for a loaf of leavened oatmeal. Later in the century people started to refer to it as a 'journey-cake'. This may be the origin of the word, but it is more probably an instance of folk etymologising—people making some sense of what otherwise makes no sense at all. How we acquired the word is not clear but it was possibly through the influence of the military in British colonies since it turns up in the West Indies as well.

In Australia the grain used was wheat and the cake was fried in the pan rather than baked. It was certainly the staple of travellers in the bush.

## jumbuck

> The following is a specimen of such eloquence: 'You pilmillally jumbuck plenty sulky me, plenty boom, borack gammon' which being interpreted means, 'If you shoot my sheep I shall be very angry, and will shoot you and no mistake.'
>
> C. Griffith, *Present State and Prospects of the Port Phillip District of New South Wales*, 1845.

Australian English has a lot of untidy etymologies acquired in its short history. One word with an uncertain origin is 'jumbuck', a sheep. Some believe that it comes from an Aboriginal language, the suggested one being Kamilaroi. Others think that it is from Aboriginal pidgin 'jump-up' derived from English. The idea here is that the sheep jump up when approached. Alternatively, the use of 'jump up' might be akin to its use in 'jumpup whitefellow' where it means in effect 'a ghost' or 'reincarnation of an Aboriginal with white skin'. In a similar way a sheep with its white fleece is thought of as being ghostly.

# (Kk)

**kangaroo**

> One of the men saw an animal something less than a greyhound; it was of a mouse colour, very slender made, and swift of foot...called by the Natives Kangooroo or Kanguru.
>
> Captain Cook's Journal, 23 June and 4 August 1770.

The first person to record this word was Captain Cook who borrowed it from the Guugu Yimidhirr, an Aboriginal tribe living near the Endeavour River in northern Queensland. The next person to visit was Captain King in 1820, and he also wrote down words from the Aboriginal language, but did not mention 'kangaroo'. Indeed, he recorded a different word entirely. As a result there was endless speculation along the lines that the Aborigines and Cook had misunderstood each other, and that when Cook asked 'What's that animal that looks like a greyhound?', the Aborigines really said, 'I don't know what you're talking about', or, even worse, gave him a rude word to take back as a joke on the white man.

In 1972 a linguist, John Haviland, studied the language again and concluded that Cook and the Guugu Yimidhirr had had a meaningful exchange and that 'kangaroo' was the Aboriginal name. The fact that the story keeps popping up shows that it is hard to put out etymological bushfires once they have started.

## kangaroo dog

We talked. Malcolm told us about his boundary riding: Boxer, his horse, and his two dogs, Butcher and Bluey, great cobbers...Butcher was a kangaroo-dog, a big dark-grey hound; ripped open once by the terrible upward kick of an 'old man' at bay, but ready to fight again as soon as his wounds were healed.

Thomas Wood, *Cobbers*, 1934.

The 'kangaroo dog' is what the English greyhound became when it was transported to Australia. Whereas greyhounds were used to chase rabbits, the 'kangaroo dog' was required to chase an animal somewhat larger and more ferocious when cornered, so there are suggestions that the greyhound was crossed with something a bit more solid, like a mastiff or a bulldog. There is evidence for this in its alternative name 'kangaroo hound'. The breed had a greyhound head with a rather more thickset body and could be any colour under the sun. In colonial times every property owner had one when hunting kangaroos was business and pleasure, and provided food for the dinner table.

## koala

Just as Australia, as a whole, lives on the sheep's back, the Australian tourist industry lives on the koala's back. But the koala (average weight 12 lb.) has a much smaller back.
Cyril Pearl, *So, You Want to Be an Australian*, 1959.

The white settlers, like most colonists, were nostalgic, backward looking, and favoured names like 'native bear' (koala), 'native dog' (dingo), 'native hedgehog' or 'native porcupine' (echidna), 'native magpie' (magpie), 'native pheasant', 'native tiger', 'native turkey', etc., which linked their new environment with their memories of home. This kind of naming was ultimately considered by the community to be unsatisfactory. The 'native bear' was not really a bear so why call it a bear? This combined with a sense that Aboriginal names for plants and animals had a greater authority. After several early colonial versions of the Aboriginal name— 'cullawine', 'coolah', 'koolah'—the anglicised 'koala' became the standard and the term 'native bear' was discarded.

## kookaburra

This gigantic dagger of a bill is the first bit of kookaburra you see. He sits hunched up on an old stump, his big domed head sunk on his chest, and his brown coat-tails drooping behind him. Now and again he chuckles to himself in Rabelaisian reminiscence.

Thomas Wood, *Cobbers*, 1934.

There are a number of words borrowed from Aboriginal languages which took a little while to settle into English because the sound systems were so different. 'Kookaburra', borrowed from the Wiradjuri language spoken in the region of the Murrumbidgee and the Lachlan, appeared as 'gogera', 'gogobera', 'cooguburra', 'cooraburra', and 'kukuburra'. For a while it all seemed too hard and English names like 'laughing jackass' and 'settler's clock' were popular. By the 1920s the preferred form 'kookaburra' had emerged, but rival spellings and pronunciations continued up to that time.

## koori

If you were koori, what chance did you have of finding a job?—except, if you were lucky, cleaning up white-feller's dirt? None at all.

Hyllus Maris and Sonia Borg, *Women of the Sun*, 1985.

Most of our borrowing from Aboriginal languages was done in the early days of white settlement but 'koori' is a later borrowing into Australian English. It made its first appearance in the 1830s as a word used by Aboriginal groups from the central coast of New South Wales. Literally, 'koori' means 'man'.

In the 1980s it gained a greater status as it seemed to many—Aborigines and non-Aborigines—that the term 'Aborigine' carried too much baggage. Also it was not particularly distinctive, since it simply means 'indigenous'. Yet attempts to make 'Koori' synonymous with 'Aborigine' foundered because of the large number of different Aboriginal groups and languages that exist in Australia.

'Koori' works for southern New South Wales and Victoria, but in parts of Queensland the term is 'Murri' and in Western Australia it is 'Nyungar'. In Arnhem Land it is 'Yolngu', in the Pilbara it is 'Mardu'. In South Australia it is 'Nunga' and in Tasmania it is 'Palawa'. What has happened as a result is that Australian English has expanded to cope with regional distinctions.

## kurdaitcha man

A kurdaitcha man could not be seen. A kurdaitcha man had magic shoes, made of emu feathers gummed together with blood; and when he put them on he left no tracks. Or if he left a track, it read the same coming as going. He could, with the proper incantations, point a bone towards a man and the man would die; even though he was a hundred miles away in the heart of another tribe.

But the kurdaitcha man could not be seen. Nobody could know his identity.

Olaf Ruhen, *Naked under Capricorn*, 1958.

---

There are many variant forms of 'kurdaitcha'—'kadaitcha', 'kaditcha', 'kooditcha', 'kadaitja' and 'goditcha'. A word that was borrowed into Australian English in the late 1800s, it hasn't yet settled down. There is even some doubt which Aboriginal language it came from, but the best guess is Arrente, the Alice Springs language. Carl Strehlow (1871–1922), missionary and linguist, suggested that, rather than being an Aboriginal word borrowed into English, it is an English word borrowed comparatively recently into the Arrente language.

The term 'kurdaitcha' also refers to the shoes which the kurdaitcha man wears. They are made from emu feathers, string made from human hair, and kangaroo fur stuck together with human blood. They afford the wearer the property of being untraceable and are worn on journeys of vengeance when it is important to frustrate the inevitable retribution. If the bringer of revenge cannot be tracked then he is safe in his mission.

The kurdaitcha spirit inhabits the man who undertakes this task and does not leave him until his mission is accomplished.

## kurrajong

What a time it would be when all the tribes gathered for this feasting. All the family would be off at the first sign that came to warn us the time had arrived. How we would wait for the kurrajong flowers to flash yellow in the sun, for the coral-tree with its red blooms to give the signal for the fish to run in the rivers and the yams to sweeten in the jungle!

W. E. Harney, *Brimming Billabongs*, 1947.

The kurrajong is a large and shapely tree with a tendency towards a bottle trunk and a convoluted pattern of branches. It seems that a number of trees were referred to as 'kurrajong' by the Aborigines because they had bark that produces the kind of fibre that could be used to make fishing lines, fishing nets and carry bags. The word 'kurrajong' comes from the Dharug and means 'fishing line'. Subsequently the broad categorisation that the Aborigines employed became the narrow labelling of the white settlers who limited its application to three kinds of *Brachychiton*, the 'red kurrajong', the 'black kurrajong' and the 'desert kurrajong'.

The kurrajong is a useful tree in that the foliage of the black kurrajong can be eaten by cattle and is fodder in times of drought. The red kurrajong and the black kurrajong have edible seeds, provided you learn the trick from the Aborigines of baking them in the ashes and removing their protective poisonous casing.

# (Ll)

**lair**

> Mr Floyd was almost always drunk. He was very flash
> and good-looking—big and weak like a boarding-house
> cup of tea, my father reckoned. Before he got married
> he used to wear gold cufflinks in the coat sleeves of his
> blue serge suit: I suppose he was what we used to call a
> lair, although he was very popular around South Perth.
> T. A. G. Hungerford, *Stories from Suburban Road*, 1983.

In cockney slang someone who is leery is 'fly', that is, someone
in the know. These days they would be regarded as being
street-wise. In the 1890s, as now, a person's street cred was
assessed on their clothes, so the 'leery cove' dressed in a way
that would identify him to his fellows, never mind if the
middle classes thought it was loud and vulgar. 'Leery' changed
to 'lairy' and acquired a noun form—'lair'. To say that

someone is 'such a lair' means you think they are showing off, although there might be a little bit of admiration in it. To describe someone as a 'mug lair' is to brand them as both vulgar and stupid. 'Mug' in that sense almost always pushes what follows in a negative direction. To 'lairise' is to behave like a lair—to show off in order to get attention.

## lamington

There were Sunday mornings in the kitchen, or Saturday afternoons if there was to be a party, when Mother and Jean and Marj would be endlessly baking— scones and sausage-rolls and sponges and cream-puffs and rock cakes and queen cakes, and sometimes a tray of lamingtons specially for me.

George Johnston, *My Brother Jack*, 1964.

An early citation for 'lamington' is from the *Guild Cookery Book* published by the Holy Trinity Ladies Working Guild in 1909. The lamington is thought to be named after Charles Wallace Baillie, Baron Lamington (1860–1940), who was Governor of Queensland from 1895 to 1901. The governor was a conservative who is remembered primarily in such placenames as Lamington Plateau in Queensland and Mount Lamington in Papua New Guinea. The cake, if it is truly named after him, would be his greatest memorial.

## larrikin

At seven o'clock Jonah and Chook arrived. They were dressed in the height of larrikin fashion—tight-fitting suits of dark cloth, soft black felt hats, and soft white shirts with new black mufflers round their necks in place of collars—for the larrikin taste in dress runs to a surprising neatness. But their boots were remarkable, fitting like a glove, with high heels and a wonderful ornament of perforated toe-caps and brass eyelet-holes on the uppers.

Louis Stone, *Jonah*, 1911.

---

Melbourne, 1869, and an Irish policeman is giving court evidence about a youth in the dock. 'He was larkin' your honour,' he says, his Irish accent seeming to make the 'r' go on for ever. 'Larrrrrrkin.' This is the folk story which gives the origin of 'larrikin' and the only pity is that there is no evidence to support it. This word appeared in Melbourne streets in the 1860s when 'larrikins' were somewhat more intimidating than we would consider them to be today. Then a larrikin was one of the gangs of youths who roamed the streets looking for trouble.

One theory is that 'larrikin' derives from 'Larry', a shortening of 'Lawrence' which was a common name among the Irish, plus '-kin', an ending meaning 'little'. So all those little Larries grew to an age where they became troublesome on the streets. Another idea is that the word evolved, not in

Melbourne, but in earlier British slang from the descriptor 'leary kinchen'. 'Leary' means 'flash, showy of dress and manners' and 'kinchen' means 'a young man'. The *English Dialect Dictionary* supports this, recording 'larrikin' to mean 'a mischievous or frolicsome youth' in the dialects of Warwickshire and Worcestershire. Whatever its origins, the word has certainly softened over time in Australia so that to be called 'a bit of a larrikin' is to be given a certain amount of respect, to be regarded as a man who can make life interesting with his exploits.

## London to a brick on

'He's going to give us the good oil. We'll be in.'

'Or out,' I said, but of course I didn't believe that myself.

'If it's on we're in,' Ambrose said, 'and it's on. London to a brick.'

T. A. G. Hungerford, *Stories from Suburban Road*, 1983.

This phrase is uniquely Australian and was popularised by Ken Howard, a well-known race caller in the 1950s. In racing parlance 'London to a brick on' is a statement of betting odds in which the punter is willing to bet London to win one brick—a bet which indicates supreme confidence. Often the phrase is shortened to just 'London to a brick'. It is a variation on a common theme with British examples such as 'bet all Lombard Street to a china orange', 'bet a million to a bit of dirt'.

### lucky country

Australia is a lucky country run mainly by second-rate people who share its luck.

Donald Horne, *The Lucky Country*, 1964.

Donald Horne's famous title for his book springs from his argument that Australia had survived up to modern times mainly on good luck rather than good management, and that we couldn't continue to rely on good luck alone in the future. Ironically, the title was then popularised with the meaning that Australia was indeed a lucky country, a land of plenty offering endless opportunity. It continues to be used in this benign way as an invocation of how fortunate Australians are.

### luderick

The first time this subject was mentioned, we were fishing for 'niggers'. The official name for 'niggers', or blackfish, is 'luderick'. They are listed as luderick on the monthly returns. But fishermen call them niggers. Niggers like to feed among mangroves, when the tide is high.

Nino Culotta, *Gone Fishin'*, 1962.

This fish is rather like a bream, with distinctive dark stripes across its back giving rise to its alternative names 'blackfish', 'black bream', 'black perch', 'darkie' and 'nigger'. 'Luderick' is now its official name, taken from the Ganay language in Victoria's Gippsland region. In New Zealand it is known as the 'mangrove fish', which confirms the predilection noted in the quote above. It is a twist of fate that has elevated the Victorian name for this fish above all its rivals, which I suspect have been dismissed because they are confusing (the fish is not a bream and not a perch) or offensive.

## lyrebird

No lyrebirds gambolled across the track to flute in eucalyptus aisles across a big singing creek.
Miles Franklin, *Childhood at Brindabella*, 1963.

Louis-Claude Desaules de Freycinet, French naval explorer, made two journeys to Australia. The first was a two-year mapping expedition in 1802, the second a much more comprehensive survey including an account of flora and fauna in 1817–18. In his *Voyage autour du Monde* (*Voyage around the World*), dated 1824, de Freycinet mentioned the bird named 'oiseau-lyre' (bird-lyre) or 'lyre magnifique' (magnificent lyre) because, as he explained, it put its tail feathers into an elegant lyre shape. The name was certainly apt, even more so because of the pun on 'liar', the bird being able to mimic any sound that it heard. For a short time in colonial days humans of a mendacious nature were referred to as 'lyrebirds'.

# (Mm)

## magpie

Country children learn early to avoid 'snakey' places in summer, and other hazards. In bush and suburbs an occasional nesting magpie 'turns really nasty'. Kids with red or fair hair seem to be more at risk from 'dive bombing maggies' than those with darker colouring.

Nancy Keesing, *Lily on the Dustbin*, 1982.

What is the explanation for 'magpie'? It is not a homegrown Australian word—there are black-and-white English birds called 'magpies' from which our 'magpie' derived its name.

The English bird was originally called a 'pie'—and by 'originally' I am talking about 1250 or thereabouts. This word came from the Latin 'pica', thought to come from the Latin verb 'pingo' meaning 'to paint or embroider, and then to stain'. It is related to the word 'pied'. By the fifteenth century the English were addressing the bird as 'Mag' which is one of the many affectionate shortenings of 'Margaret', in much the same fashion as we call the wagtail 'Willy'. In time, 'Mag pie' fused to 'magpie'.

The European settlers took one look at our bird and thought 'magpie', but, in fact, the English bird belongs to the crow family, whereas our 'magpie', along with its cousin the butcherbird, is in a distinct family of its own.

**magsman**

'He's a quiet one,' Barbie said. 'All right in a dust-up, though. No magsman at all.'

D'Arcy Niland, *Call Me When the Cross Turns Over*, 1957.

'Magsman' in Australian English refers to a man who has the gift of the gab, who can talk fluently and, more often than not, longer than his audience considers desirable. An earlier meaning is 'confidence man', since an ability to mesmerise a listener was an essential skill for such a person. In 1838 an English newspaper commented that 'A magsman must, of necessity be a great actor, and a most studious observer of human nature'. The word survived into the early 1900s as a general colloquialism even though it was no longer a term used by criminals. It is derived from the verb 'to mag' or chatter incessantly. This is from Yorkshire and northern British dialects and is an abbreviated form of 'magpie', the English magpie being a noisy bird.

## makarrata

Makarrata is a Yolngu word for agreement. It signifies the end of a dispute between communities or between a community and an offender, and the resumption of normal relations.

Aboriginal Treaty Committee, 1980.

This word is an example of a conscious effort to introduce a new word into Australian English, something that is extremely difficult to do. 'Makarrata' trembled on the brink of acceptance throughout the 1980s, but never quite broke through into our national awareness. In the last few decades we have had many significant Aboriginal or Aboriginal-related additions as encyclopedic entries to the dictionary—'Barunga statement', 'Mabo', 'Wik' and 'post-Wik', and more recently 'Sorry Day'. In all of this, 'makarrata' has slipped from favour, succeeded by broad references to 'reconciliation' or specific references to a 'peace treaty'. The English forms now seem preferable to the Aboriginal borrowing, possibly because they need no explanation.

## mallee

> I unyoked with despatch, then left the bullocks, and
> rode round, looking for a clump of mallee, which would
> indicate the immediate neighbourhood of the water.
>
> Joseph Furphy, *Such Is Life*, 1903.

The word 'mallee' is thought to have been borrowed from the
language Wembawemba spoken in western Victoria. The term
is used for any of various eucalypts which have a distinctive
habit of growth—the branches all shoot from close to the
ground, springing from a common base called a lignotuber.
The tree stores starch in the lignotuber, possibly to protect it
from fire. The lignotuber is known as the 'mallee root' and
presented a huge obstacle to settlers wishing to farm mallee
land because of the difficulty in digging it out.

It is not uncommon in Australia to label broad areas by the
type of vegetation, so the land covered in mallee became 'the
mallee'. In addition to this we have 'the brigalow', 'the
pindan', 'the spinifex' and 'the lignum'. 'Brigalow' is possibly
from Kamilaroi in eastern New South Wales. 'Pindan' is from
the Bardi word *bindan*, Bardi being the language spoken in
northern Western Australia, north of Broome. The plant
genus *Spinifex* was named by Carl von Linné (Carolus
Linnaeus) who blended the Latin *spina* meaning 'spine' with
the suffix *-fex* denoting 'a maker', from *facere* meaning 'to
make'. Finally, 'lignum' is a shortening of the botanical name
Polygonum, a family of plants with slender tangled stems,

forming in swamps a dense thicket and found in lignum swamps throughout Australia.

### marsupial

> They say there are compensations for living in Van Diemen's Land—some very quaint marsupials.
>
> Patrick White, *A Fringe of Leaves*, 1976.

The Latin *marsupium* means 'a pouch', and the family Marsupiala is named from the characteristic pouch in which the young are carried. The zoological nomenclature became part of the ordinary naming practice of colonial Australia, so that we have terms such as 'marsupial lion' (an extinct animal of the genus *Thylacine)*, 'marsupial mole', 'marsupial mouse', 'marsupial rat' and 'marsupial wolf' (otherwise known as the 'Tasmanian tiger'). The logic of the naming pattern is that the animal looks like a known mammal but is of the marsupial kind.

### mate

> These men when they contract to do heavy work, as clearing, fencing, etc. almost always do it in parties of two, or more, being prompted to this in the first place by the hardness of the work, which a man cannot face alone, requiring always the assistance of 'neighbours',

or 'mates', or 'partners', as they are severally called, even in the minute details.

A. Maconochie, *Thoughts on Convict Management*, 1838.

The history of 'mate' in Australian English is a good illustration that it's not what you do but the way that you do it. This means that it doesn't matter so much where the words come from but rather what we as a community make them mean once we have them. 'Mate' is a word in British English and American English. For us, though, the meaning goes much deeper than just 'partner' or 'comrade', 'buddy' or 'pal'. In the struggles of settlement 'mates' were men who worked as partners, often in a longstanding commitment, to perform difficult and dangerous work such as fencing, land clearing, goldmining—jobs that were well nigh impossible to do on your own. The bush was a dangerous place and it was safer to work in pairs. Then the 'mates' went to war and the word was imbued with wartime heroism and suffering. And now? 'Mate' has very little real meaning left, but it is still a powerful word in our vocabulary with its affirmation of trust.

### melaleuca

The tea-tree of the colonists belongs to the beautiful genus *Melaleuca*, of which there are many species in Australia, though only two have been found in other parts of the world.

R. Mudie, *The Picture of Australia*, 1829.

The melaleuca should perhaps have acquired the common name 'the black and white tree'. It was named by Carolus Linnaeus who in 1767 established the two-level system of scientific naming for plants and animals called the Linnean System. So the melaleuca was one plant that Joseph Banks would have known what to call when he identified it in Australia. Its botanical name comes from the Greek 'melas' black and 'leucos' white. The tree was known throughout Asia and it was noticeable for its white bark blackened in patches by fire. The cajuput, a tree of the same family, gets its name from the Malay 'kayu' wood and 'putih' white.

Captain Cook's crew called our melaleuca the 'tea-tree', because they made tea with its small leaves, as did the settlers who followed them. At that time the tea was described as 'too highly aromatic to please the European taste'.

## messmate

The route wound through bold outcrops of copper coloured hills, over stony, treeless vistas—hard country, unfolding into open plains with welcome belts of messmate and shady silver box.

Mary Durack, 'On to the Territory' in *Twenty-Four*, 1959.

In the Middle Ages a type of banquet was arranged where four people sat at each table and were served together from the same dish of food (or 'mess'). This grouping was then called a 'mess'. It was preserved in the Inns of Court for the legal fraternity. Later the army and the navy adopted the term for each of the several parties into which a regiment of a ship's company was divided, the members of which ate together. And so, in general use, a messmate was a companion of long standing, one with whom you might regularly share your meals.

J. H. Maiden, an Australian botanist of the early 1900s, reported that the tree known as 'messmate' always grew with other kinds of stringybark in an association reminiscent of bosom companions. Another story is that messmate was a good choice of companion when you were setting up the campfire because the bark it shed was useful to start the fire.

## min min

Boulia is a nice little far-west Queensland town, with the Min-Min Store (named for the famous min min 'ghost' light of the area).
*Australian Women's Weekly*, December 1981.

Along with the 'bunyip' we have the 'mindi', also from the Wembawemba of western Victoria. The 'mindi' is a large mythical snake which lies in wait beside waterholes. The snake is supposedly hairy, although no one has seen it for the simple reason that if you see it you die. Such is its power. It is also recorded as being able to spit its poison. The Aboriginal people regarded smallpox as 'mindi dust'.

The 'min min' is a spirit of a different order from a different region. It is said to be from a language in the Cloncurry area of Queensland, yet no one can find the word in any of the local Aboriginal languages and the last speakers of these languages did not recognise it. The 'min min' is a will-o'-the-wisp, a mysterious light that floats above the plains. It is described as being like a car light without throwing a beam, and has been variously explained away as methane gas from the local bores, ball lightning, the glow of nocturnal insects, and the emanations of certain types of fungus. All the evidence for the 'min min light' is comparatively recent—from the mid-1900s—and may be generated by a local desire to have a tourist attraction. Have you noticed how many towns claim to have the original black stump?

## mob

It was the light that prevailed, and distance, which, after all, was a massing of light, and the mobs of cockatoos, which exploded, and broke into flashes of clattering, shrieking, white and sulphur light.

Patrick White, *Voss*, 1957.

The starting point for the word 'mob' is its meaning in British English as a rabble. In the bush this was transferred to groups of Aborigines regarded as wild and hostile, and then to groups of animals, as in 'a big mob of cattle'. Later the threatening connotation faded and the sense of large numbers became predominant. A 'mob' could refer to any group with some connecting link or shared characteristic. The group could be big—the 'Melbourne mob' as opposed to the 'Sydney mob', or small—'my mob', meaning 'my family'. In Aboriginal English this use of 'mob' can be with reference to the whole community linked by language and culture. An interesting twist in this word's use is the shift from its reference to a large number of items whether they be people, cattle, goods or whatever, to 'a large quantity of something' as in 'I like big mobs of butter on my toast'.

## mollydooker

...fork-hander, mauldy and mollydooker, a left-handed boxer (taken from old English 'mauley' and 'dook' or 'duke', the fist or hand).

Sidney J. Baker, *The Australian Language*, 1966.

A left-hander is a 'mollydooker' or sometimes simply a 'molly-dook'. The first part of this word is probably the same word which appears in 'mollycoddle'. In British dialect a 'molly' was a fussy man who did what was regarded as women's work. The 'dook' part is slang meaning a hand or fist. This is now still used in the jocular invitation to fight: 'put up your dooks'. Apparently it comes from the rhyming slang 'Duke (or 'Dook') of Yorks' for 'forks'. 'Forks' was old thieves' slang for fingers or hands. When you put these two elements together you get 'mollydooker', a weak-handed person. Not that left-handed people are really weak-handed at all, yet there has been this prejudice with us from time immemorial. In the Indo-European culture, from which Western culture developed, the 'right' was considered lucky and the 'left' unlucky. In fact, the word for 'left' is very different in all Indo-European languages which signifies that the original word was taboo and had to be replaced by another less offensive word from time to time. For instance, the Latin word for left is 'sinister' which also meant evil and unlucky. Another example of this derogatory notion applied to the left is the surfing term 'goofy-footed' originally used to describe a left-footed surfer, and nowadays also used for left-footed snowboarders.

## mongrel

You can, of course, always tell St Kilda supporters. The club might be broke, the management in disarray, the coach reaching for the Valium, and the team a fearful

> 27 goals behind going into the last quarter. But as one,
> we unite and scream: 'You mongrel umpire!!!!'
> *Sun* (Melbourne), 1988.

The base meaning of 'mongrel' is a dog of mixed breeding and from this beginning many metaphors have flowed. 'You mongrel!' was a line of abuse in British English which fell out of use there just as it was handed down to colonial Australia. On the other hand, Australian English took the mongrel ball and ran with it. We used it as direct invective—it appears in the writings of Joseph Furphy ('You mongrel!') and Henry Lawson ('You mongrel person!'). The expression 'a mongrel act' is one that is embedded in Australian culture. And as we can see from the quote above, used epithetically the term is alive and well. The other sense of the adjective—of mixed origin—also survives. As followers of Aussie Rules will know, a 'mongrel kick' is one that started out as one thing and finished up as another with unpleasing results.

### monotreme

It is rather surprising that the spiny ant-eater, or echidna, is not as famous as the platypus, for it is just as interesting and just as odd. It is the only other member of the very primitive group of monotremes, and it is in Australia and New Guinea alone that these two egg-laying mammals are to be found.

Lyla Stevens, *Animals of Australia in Colour*, 1956.

Etienne Geoffroy Saint-Hilaire (1772–1844) became, at the age of twenty-one, the professor of zoology at the Museum of Natural History in Paris. He was a precursor to Darwin in that he believed new species might arise from occasional mutations flourishing in a new environment.

He studied Australian mammals collected by the naturalist François Péron who accompanied Baudin in his expedition 1800–04. Saint-Hilaire named this strange new group of animals from the Greek *mono* meaning 'one' and *trema* meaning 'hole', a reference to the characteristic single opening for reproductive and excretory functions. The order of mammals he called Monotremata. The anglicised form 'monotreme' is the common name for members of this order.

## mulga

Time passed and patients began to dawdle in: 'news was noised around'. 'Mulga wires' travel miraculously in the Inland.

Ion L. Idriess, *Flynn of the Inland*, 1932.

This word is from the Yuwaalarraay language spoken by Aboriginals near Lightning Ridge in New South Wales. It is applied to a number of different kinds of acacia which are a feature of the dry inland terrain. They are mostly shrubby in height and shape and seem to dominate the landscape. Thus the expression 'the mulga' is a synonym for the outback. Briefly 'mulga' was the equivalent of 'bushie', as in 'There were a few mulgas at the party in their big boots and broad-brim hats', but that use has not survived.

'Mulga' has combined to form 'mulga country', 'mulga paddocks', 'mulga flats'. In this sense it means 'countrified', as in 'My mulga mates really stick out in a group of city slickers'. The 'mulga wire' is the equivalent of the bush telegraph, although sometimes it seemed to refer to smoke signals. 'Mulga madness' is the lunacy that overtakes you when you live out the back of nowhere. And the 'mulga mafia' would these days be described as 'agri-politicians'.

### muster

The boss last night in the hut did say,
'We start to muster at break of day;
So be up first thing, and don't be slow;
Saddle your horses and off you go.'
Anon, 'Mustering Song', date unknown.

In the military world a 'muster' occurred when all the soldiers assembled. In the Australian context it first meant an assembly of convicts and then later, as military structures and systems were imposed on the organisation of agriculture, the rounding up of cattle for counting and branding. On a large station finding out how many head of cattle you had was a big undertaking but it needed to be done at regular intervals. A 'bangtail muster' was one in which the tails of the cattle were banged or docked as they were counted so that it was possible to tell them apart from the uncounted.

## myall

A lazy smile crossed Dusty's face. 'Sadie comes from myall black fella tribe y'u know.'
'What means myall?'
'She's wild.'

Wal Watkins, *Andamooka*, 1971.

In this excerpt the Chinese cook is addressing a donkey which he has unsuccessfully been trying to break in. This quote is a perfect example of the way 'myall' would be used in Aboriginal English. The donkey is wild, but, more than that, it is unteachable. It refuses to have anything to do with the civilised world in which it is meant to be a docile beast of burden. In Aboriginal English 'myall' has bad connotations and in some situations can be the equivalent of 'stupid'.

In Australian English 'myall' is the opposite of 'tame'. People described as 'myalls' live in the bush, rarely visit settlements, and remain wholly immersed in the traditional

Aboriginal way of life. A 'myall' occasions a degree of respect, along with considerable wariness because they are operating on a different set of ground rules. The word 'myall' is from the Dharug language and meant 'stranger'. Both Aborigines and white settlers then applied it to any Aborigine that came from beyond the borders of settlement.

It is also applied to wild animals or those that go wild, as in 'myall cattle'. And it is the name of a species of acacia with a hard fine-grained wood used for carving. There is uncertainty about the way in which this tree was named but one theory is that the Kamilaroi supplied this wood to the Dharug. They were regarded by them as 'myalls', that is, 'strangers', and the wood they provided was referred to as 'myall wood'.

**myxo, the**

> We used to find a possum once in every hollow spout
> On all the river-gums before the myxo thinned them
> out.
> The fellows on the PP Boards will claim it isn't true,
> It killed the rabbits, I believe, and killed the possums
> too.
>
> Keith Garvey, 'The Possum' in
> *Absolutely Australian*, 1979.

'Myxomatosis' is the name of a virus which occurs naturally in South America and which causes a fatal illness in rabbits. To Australians of the postwar generation this word is significant because of its dramatic effect on the rabbit population here. The possibility of using 'myxomatosis' was investigated in the 1920s but it was not until the 1950s that it was released. In true Australian fashion the name was rapidly shortened to 'the myxo'.

# (Nn)

## namma hole

When white men came to give their horses water for a few days, the natives found to their dismay that the waters had dried away; for the well was only a rock hole that had filled with sand, and once the water was drained out nothing remained. Those desert wells were called 'namma holes', and how they were first found I do not know.

W. E. Harney, *Brimming Billabongs*, 1947.

---

A 'namma hole' is another intriguing phenomenon of the Australian bush. It is a hole in a rock which has filled with water. Sometimes, though the opening may be quite small, the rock can be hollowed out to some depth.

It has been suggested that 'namma' is an Aboriginal word for a woman's breast. This seems appropriate, both because it conveys the shape of the indentation in the rock and the dependency of the people on the water which it contains.

While it is agreed that the word is from the Nyungar language, spoken over a wide area of south-western Western Australia, this explanation of its origin has been dismissed as fanciful, though no better one has been offered.

## nankeen kestrel

Billy snatched the newspaper with a shout of exaspera-tion, causing a little nankeen kestrel hunting lizards along the track to wheel away in alarm.

Jack Bennett, *Gallipoli*, 1981.

The original 'nankeen' was a yellow cotton from Nanking, now Nanjing, a seaport in eastern China. The Anglicisation of foreign words usually throws up a number of variant spellings in the early stages, particularly when the original language is as remote from English as Chinese. The cloth made from this cotton was popular in the late 1700s but was eventually made elsewhere from ordinary cotton and dyed yellow. Trousers of nankeen were still popular in the early 1800s, even in the colonies.

Nankeen is a light yellow or pale buff colour. The nankeen kestrel, found throughout Australia, is pale rufous on its upper parts. There is also a nankeen bird or night-heron which is described as cinnamon-coloured. And Mary Durack in *Kings in Grass Castles* mentions a nankeen plover which is a harbinger of drought.

## nardoo

The fish being disposed of, next came a supply of nardoo cake and water until I was so full as to be unable to eat any more; when Pitchery, allowing me a short time to recover myself, fetched a large bowl of the raw nardoo flour mixed to a thin paste, a most insinuating article, and one that they appear to esteem a great delicacy.

William Wills, diary, Cooper Creek, 1861.

The 'nardoo' is a small fern that grows in swamps and waterways with its clover-like fronds floating on the surface. It is one of the most widely distributed Aboriginal plant foods; its spore cases contain starch and are ground into a flour. Mixed with water this becomes a paste that can be eaten on its own or cooked as a damper. This is, however, food that is eaten as a last resort since there is little nutritional value in the nardoo flour.

The Aboriginal name 'ngardu' occurs in a number of languages over a wide area of South Australia, south-west Queensland and western New South Wales. Its transfer into

Australian English seems to have been with Burke and Wills who were fed nardoo at Cooper Creek in South Australia, although it didn't do them much good.

### nark

It is a curious fact that so much which goes to make up Australia cannot be defined positively, but only in terms of opposition to the wowser, the eternal grey nark, born without balls, guts or gullet, slimy and sanctimonious, a figure to be pitied and pilloried.

*Snatches and Lays*, S. Hogbotel and S. Ffuckes eds, 1973.

Narks and wowsers are often lumped together as 'undesirables' of our culture, and may well be linked with those two great evils, whingeing and dobbing. In British dialect 'to nark someone' is 'to exasperate or irritate them'. We can trace 'nark' to a German word meaning 'to grate'. In British English a 'nark' is a person who rubs you up the wrong way. For us a 'nark' is rather more than that. From a momentary irritation this person proceeds to make a life's habit of picking on others and spoiling everyone's fun. A 'copper's nark' is 'an informer'—can it get any worse?

## neenish tart

Method: Roll out very thin and bake in patty tins. Fill
with mock cream when cold, then ice half the tart with
chocolate icing, and the other half with white icing.

*The Orange Recipe Gift Book*, 1925.

---

Another of life's little lexical mysteries is the 'Neenish tart'.
The first puzzle is over the spelling—'nenish', 'neenish' or
'nienish', capitalised or not? Those who support the Nienish
spelling argue a Viennese or German origin. But there is a
strong counterclaim from a Mrs Evans of Grong Grong, New
South Wales, who maintains that in 1913 her mother's friend,
Ruby Neenish, ran out of cocoa whilst baking up a batch of
tarts for her daughter's unexpected shower tea.

Staying cool, calm, collected and creative in the kitchen in
this extreme emergency, Ruby had the bright idea of using
chocolate icing for one half of the tart and white icing for the
other. Her creation was immortalised in the *Orange Recipe Gift
Book* and reproduced by countless other grateful cooks. This
may be just a good story, of course, but at the moment it's the
best we've got, and the residents of Orange are sticking to it.

## Never-Never, the

Out at Meekatharra in Western Australia Barry (B.F.)
Murphy had just driven his team of beautiful tall camels

150 miles in from the Never-Never country where the small copper mines were providing him with so much ore to cart that he and his 14-camel team were kept occupied all year round.

Patsy Adam-Smith, *The ANZACS*, 1978.

E. E. Morris's *Austral English* (1898) has an entry for 'Never, Never Country' dating back to 1857, which claims that it is an anglicisation of an Aboriginal word meaning 'unoccupied country'. There is, however, no support for this. Another explanation, that this is country from which you will never never come back, seems more reasonable. The 'Never-Never' is specifically North Queensland but in general use could be taken as a synonym for the Outback.

This is one word that transferred from Australian English back to British English. In *Peter Pan* (1904), Peter explains that children who fall out of their prams go to Never Never land. In the early 1900s the term had gained the meaning of an imaginary and Utopian land, presumably an idealisation of the wilderness. In this rosy glow, the Never-Never becomes an Australian version of Shangri-la.

**new chum**

In the colony I've just arrived,
My togs, I know, look rum;

> And you can see with half an eye
> That I'm a green new-chum.
>> Charles R. Thatcher, 'Green New-Chum', c. 1850s.

This expression has little left in it of its original meaning and connotation. James Hardy Vaux in his *Flash Language* (1819) explains that a 'chum' was a fellow prisoner in a jail or hulk. 'New chums' are the newcomers, 'old chums' are the old hands, so in the Australian context the new chum was the new arrival. It could also mean 'novice'—new chums on the goldfields were not just newly arrived but inexperienced miners. 'Chum' itself goes back to British English of the late 1600s and referred to someone with whom you shared rooms, perhaps at boarding school or students' quarters. There is also a suggestion that it is a shortened form of 'chamber mate', a piece of seventeenth-century student slang.

## no good to Gundy

'No good to Gundy'…This is the only explanation of its origin I could discover: A mounted constable was bringing a darky named Gundy down to Bathurst for trial…In the same carriage were some young men who procured much whisky at Wellington…and when one of the boys playfully held the bottle about a foot in front of the aboriginal's nose and begged of him 'Do

have a drop', Gundy threw one black foot in the air, and
deftly kicking the bottle of whisky through the carriage
window, yelled 'No plurry good to Gundy'.
        *Bulletin*, 19 December 1908.

The *Bulletin* in 1906 very knowledgeably suggested that
'gundy' was a Welsh word meaning 'to steal' and that
something 'no good to gundy' was not even worth pinching.
A year later in 1907 the same paper asserted that 'gundy' was
short for 'Gundagai' and that the expression originated in the
big flood of 1852. A bullocky who had escaped the flood,
looked back at where Gundagai used to be and remarked
sadly, 'Tweren't no good to Gundy'. A touching story.

Neither of these explanations is true—they merely reveal
a desperate search for a folk etymology. The popularity of this
expression is fading, possibly because we have no sense of
what it means.

## nong

Remember that turn in Balmain ten years ago, when
you unwittingly served up that Camembert straight out
of the fridge? Some red hot communist sheila, who
owned five homes and a string of pearls as big as
golfballs, laughed at you, and you felt a right nong.
Never done it again, even though you're a Kraft

Cheddar man in your heart of hearts.
Barry Dickins, *What the Dickins*, 1985.

There is no shortage of Aussie words for an idiot, among which 'nong' is central. It combines a firm assessment of clear-cut stupidity with a degree of tolerance. No one suspects a 'nong' of being deliberately obstructive or of having any kind of evil intent. Their stupidity is innocent though irredeemable.

Compare the simple 'nong' with other Australian put-downs: the 'ratbag' is nonconformist, socially unreliable; the 'drongo' is ploddingly boring; the 'mug alec' is brash; the 'galah' is noisy. The 'nong', meanwhile, is simple-hearted and simple-minded.

The word is a shortening of the Yorkshire 'ning-nang' which means 'a worthless or troublesome person, especially one who is constantly complaining'. It entered Australian English as military slang from World War II.

**norks**

'You know my wild days are over, Ralph,' he said, then softened the rebuke with, 'You are the playboy these days.' It was not the reaction Ralph had hoped for. He tried again, 'Sancha showed me a school photograph of her. She's not bad-looking. Tall, blonde, big norks...'

His voice trailed away, for Kanan had averted his face.
Blanche d'Alpuget, *Turtle Beach*, 1981.

---

The earliest evidence found for this word is in Criena Rohan's 1960s novel *The Delinquents* in which a man is heard to say to the young widgie protagonist, 'Hello, honey, that sweater— one deep breath and your norks will be in my soup.' This really sets the scene for the word quite perfectly, for 'norks' has always been a word used by the leering male, along with 'knockers', 'hooters', etc. It's not a slang word that women use themselves, as 'boobs' and 'tits' are.

Sidney J. Baker recorded the word in 1966 and suggested that it arose from a shortening of 'Norco', a well-known brand of butter which had a picture of a cow with a large udder on the wrapper. There is no real evidence to support Baker's conjecture, and no explanation of why they weren't first called 'norcos' before being shortened to 'norks'. Nor does it explain the occasional variant 'norgs'. Depending on your attitude to this word you will be either glad or saddened at the news that the word is dying out, and is almost unknown among the younger generation.

# (Oo)

## ocker

> The contrast between the dignified, clean, well-behaved, disciplined Vietnamese and their children and the surrounding 'ocker' Australians could not have been greater. The men, with their big bellies hanging over their belts, were drinking beer, throwing beer cans into the harbour.
>
> Geoffrey Blainey, *All for Australia*, 1984.

We owe this word to the 1960s television program 'The Mavis Bramston Show', which introduced characters devised by Ron Frazer and played by Barry Creyton ('Ocker') and Ron Frazer ('Jack'). 'Jack' constantly called 'Ocker' by name, the likely reason why it has stuck in our minds as the stereotype of boorish behaviour. Both these characters behaved in the fashion that has now been typified as 'ockerish'—loud, ignorant, bigoted and beer-swilling.

Within the English tradition of abbreviating names, 'Oscar' invariably becomes 'Ocker'. In Australian English 'ocker' has negative connotations, 'Aussie' or 'Ozzie' being the word that favours what we like about Australian men—that they be fair dinkum, unpretentious, and winners in sport.

## old man

> Every police trooper in the colony'll be after us like a pack of dingoes after an old man kangaroo when the ground's boggy...
>
> Rolf Boldrewood, *Robbery under Arms*, 1889.

This expression is often used adjectivally as in 'old-man kangaroo' or 'old-man saltbush'. An old man has authority and deserves respect. And so something large or matured, or someone in a position of power can be seen as having 'old-man' status. In British English in the 1600s, the main tunnel of a mine was referred to as 'the old man', a use which stayed with miners and was used in goldmining in Australia.

British English of the early 1800s referred to someone in authority, particularly the captain of a ship, as 'the old man', which may explain how the usage moves off into the colonies and then spreads with much greater freedom to animals and plants ('old-man crocodile', 'old-man willow'), then to things ('old-man paddock', 'old-man allotment', and of course, in

America, 'old-man river'). It had greater general use in earlier Australian English in expressions like 'old-man Christmas duff' and 'old-man spree'. These days it seems to be limited in its use to set expressions with animals and plants.

**onya**

'Dropped in on Towner today.'
'Oh, good onya mate.'
'Yeah, he was a roole egg.'
Gabrielle Carey and Kathy Lette, *Puberty Blues*, 1979.

Sometimes it is of vital importance to capture pronunciation in spelling because the significance lies in that particular utterance. The expression 'good onya, mate', often abbreviated to just 'onya', is the authentic Australianism. That other phrase, 'good on you, mate' belongs somewhere else and tugs at no patriotic heartstrings. Other such Australianisms are 'bewdy' and 'good-o' and 'g'day'. Such phrases were natural enough when they first became popular but have now acquired an edge of self-conscious nationalism.

# (Pp)

**paddock**

The stocks increased, and there was need for more pasture. Paddocks had to be cleared and fenced; trees were ring-barked and grubbed, suckers cut: the bush was forever trying to reclaim the land.

Hyllus Maris and Sonia Borg, *Women of the Sun*, 1985.

A 'paddock' in British English was a small field or enclosure, so how did it become the vast expanse of land with no visible fence that it is in parts of Australia?

Looking at the evidence in print, it would seem that it was by a process of gradual expansion. The first Australian 'paddock' mentioned in 1808 is the English 'paddock'—a small enclosure. The next one, in 1809, is eight hectares. The next, in 1819, is 215 hectares, 'fenced in with a 5-rail fence'. By 1849 the 'paddock' had expanded to 'many thousands of acres' and the writer feels compelled to acknowledge that 'no enclosed tract of land is too large to be designated "a paddock" in these colonies'.

It is as if constrained, corseted England gave a huge sigh of relief, loosed her stays and expanded visibly into the wide expanses of Australia. An Australian creek was the equivalent of an English river, and an Australian paddock was more land than the average property owner in England could ever have imagined.

## pakapoo ticket

He had come down early to mark a pak-ah-pu ticket at the Chinaman's in Hay Street.

Louis Stone, *Jonah*, 1911.

The original 'packapoo ticket' was part of a Chinese gambling game employing slips of paper marked with columns of Chinese characters. The Chinese name *pai ko p'aio* meant 'white pigeon ticket' which, it is suggested, referred to a Cantonese competition that involved the release of pigeons. A person playing the game would buy one of these tickets with a range of characters and then mark off their chosen set, in a fashion similar to Lotto but using characters rather than numbers.

A pakapoo ticket was indecipherable to most colonial

European customers so the term came to be applied to illegible handwriting or any document difficult to read.

## pavlova

I do not knock traditional Australian cooking—didn't we invent the lamington? No, we did not invent the pavlova and neither did our New Zealand cousins, though they, like us, cling to this mistaken belief.
Nancy Keesing, *Lily on the Dustbin*, 1982.

It comes as a shock to realise that this all-Australian dessert was in fact first given its name in New Zealand. The great ballerina Anna Pavlova toured Australasia in 1926, providing the occasion for the creation of this new dish. 'Light as meringue, light as whipped cream', you can hear the chef saying. The first citation is from a New Zealand 1927 booklet put out by Davis Gelatine called *Davis Dainty Dishes*.

## pea

'Do you know what this next winner is going to be?' I asked, to change the subject. 'Dunno,' answered Steak. 'Woggo will tell you when the time comes. Here he is now.'
Woggo strolled into view and halted before us. Fixing his gaze on the horizon, he slowly stroked his left ear

with three fingers, spat aimlessly in the general direction of the betting-ring and moved on. Maureen and Daisy hurriedly turned the pages of their race books. 'Useless Annie!' they gasped in unison. 'What about her?' I queried, looking around. 'That's it,' gabbled Eggs. 'That's the pea…'

Lennie Lower, *Here's Luck*, 1930.

---

This is not the legume but the colloquialism meaning 'favourite' or 'one picked to win', as in, 'I reckon that Meatpie is the pea in the 2.30.'

This meaning of 'pea' goes back to the conjurer's trick done with a pea and three thimbles. After a certain amount of hocus-pocus and swapping around of the thimbles, someone from the audience is invited to pick which thimble has the pea under it. All the while the pea has been neatly concealed in the hand of the conjurer and never under a thimble at all.

This idea of picking the 'pea' transferred to horseracing with the particular sense of being a horse that is ridden to win. The selection of the 'pea' is dependent on what you can ascertain about the intention of the owners.

More broadly 'pea' simply means the candidate most likely to succeed as for a job or promotion or the like.

## pedal wireless

First thing Monday morning our host, on his old-type pedal wireless, sent off the message about the break-down. Roy Norton, poised over the transmitter, his legs and feet working the pedals like steam pistons, roared the words breathlessly into the set...

Coralie and Leslie Rees, *Spinifex Walkabout*, 1953.

The 'pedal wireless' was a simple radio transceiver and generator that was operated by a pedal arrangement like a bicycle. It was invented by an Adelaide engineer, Alfred Traeger, in 1925. His first customer was John Flynn who wanted it for the Royal Flying Doctor Service. The set was then widely used from the 1930s throughout the outback, notably for the School of the Air. Messages sent by this means were said to have been heard 'on the pedal', and people 'pedalled the news' to each other.

## pialla

Several years after that, White Massa sent messages and tried to persuade the chiefs to forgive Mundo and Billabong Jenny, and to admit them again into the tribe. He thought that he had succeeded; but the law of the Blacks is not lightly to be set aside, and in due course there came a command to Mundo to attend a great

corroboree. Then Mundo was afraid, though he still felt
that a white medicine man who could pialla Debil-debil
in a dream might have power with the native elders.

Marilyn Lake and Katie Holmes, *Freedom Bound*,
1995.

---

First Fleeter David Collins described the pidgin English in
use at Botany Bay as 'a barbarous mixture of English with the
Port Jackson dialect'. That dialect was Dharug from which
'pialla' meaning 'to talk' is borrowed. This early pidgin
became the basis for the varieties of Aboriginal English that
exist today.

In English 'pialla' had different forms—'pai-alla', 'pialler',
'pile', 'piola'. This variation, possibly reflecting different
attempts to capture the sound of the Dharug *bayala*, would no
doubt have given way to one standard form if the word had
gained a permanent place in Australian English. It seemed
always to retain its pidgin context and flavour, however, and
did not survive colonial times.

Two other words of pidgin which failed to survive colonial
times were 'baal' used as a negative, as in 'Baal me!' meaning
'It wasn't me!', and 'bingy', pronounced 'bin-jee', meaning
'stomach'.

## piccaninny dawn

The piccaninny dawn was growing up fast. First in its strange other-world way it had become temporarily darker, then quite suddenly, the sky, and all the world became grey. Next pale grey. Then there was light. It was daybreak.

Lucy Walker, *Runaway Girl*, 1975.

'Piccaninny' is one of those colonial crossovers, hailing from the Portuguese 'pequenino' meaning 'small'. The word became part of the pidgin of the West Indies and West Africa with the meaning 'black child' and survives in West African English as 'pickin' and in Jamaican English as 'pickney', both meaning 'a small child'.

The British had interests alongside the Portuguese in the West Indies and transferred the word into the Australian context and into Australian pidgin. The colonial use of 'piccaninny' for an Aboriginal child came to be regarded as patronising and offensive.

These days it is not so much offensive as irrelevant—a word that has disappeared from use. It is unclear whether the 1900s term 'piccaninny dawn' or 'piccaninny daylight' for the uncertain or 'little' light that appears before the sun comes up can survive the stigma of 'piccaninny'. In a sense it is a better description than 'false dawn', which somehow suggests that we have all been cheated.

## pig-root

> The headmaster is appalled. He fears sentiment and
> mentally pig-roots like a nervous horse.
> > Thea Astley, *A Kindness Cup*, 1974.

The earlier form of this word was 'pig-jump'—to jump as a pig
does with all four legs straight out and not tucked under as
happens with a buckjumper. The Americans call it 'crow-
hopping', the South Africans 'pronking' (borrowed from
Afrikaans). In all cases the effect is that the horse's back is
arched and the four legs straight with knees locked. Our 'pig-
jump' first appeared in the late 1800s and by the 1900s had
been transformed into 'pig-root'.

## platypus

> On still nights when our floaters sat motionlessly in a
> moonlight path on the water, the dark surface at our feet
> would glitter with ripples then break and for a moment
> a platypus would be floating there, watching us with
> sharp eyes before it curved its body and returned to its
> burrow among the submerged roots of the old tree.
> > Alan Marshall, *I Can Jump Puddles*, 1955.

The naturalist George Shaw is credited with coining the term
'platypus' in 1799, from word elements derived from ancient
Greek. It means 'flat-footed', a deliberate reference to the
expanded webs of the platypus' front feet. Another naturalist

studying the animal, a German, J. F. Blumenbach, coined another word from ancient Greek, which pointed to one of the platypus' unique features. Blumenbach came up with the term 'ornithorhynchus', which can be translated as 'bird-nosed' or 'bird-billed'.

The word 'ornithorhynchus' is, however, quite a mouthful and so 'platypus' caught on with the general public, and 'ornithorhynchus' ended up as the scientific genus name. 'Platypus' couldn't be used as a scientific name in any case, because it had already been reserved for a type of beetle.

The early settlers also invented some other names for this creature which are no longer used, such as 'duck mole', 'water mole' and the 'paradox', this last referring to its mix of bird and animal features.

## Pommy

Admittedly, some of Harry's ancestor worship is a defence against those at Bathurst—and elsewhere—who thought he was a 'Pommy'. 'I'm a fifth-generation Australian,' Harry will say when he is baited for allegedly un-Australian attitudes, 'and I'm tired of having to be a pioneer.'

Dal Stivens, *A Horse of Air*, 1986.

It is a sad fact that folk etymologies are often more satisfying than the true explanation. Poms were not 'Prisoners of Mother England' however intuitively we respond to the image of them in the convict garb with 'POME' stamped on it. The real origin is that 'Pommy' is short for 'pomegranate'. This may conjure up the shining red cheeks of the newcomers from England, but the appeal lay as much in the possible rhyme with 'immigrant' as with anything else.

The early 1800s produced the rhyming slang 'Jimmy Grant' as the nickname for an immigrant. By the early 1900s this had transformed to 'pommygrant' or 'pommygranates'. The immigrants were still not amused. Little did they know that 'Pommy bastard' and 'whingeing Pom' lay ahead.

# (Qq)

## quokka

Exactly what is a quokka? It is...one of the smallest
members of the kangaroo group, known as macropods.
The grey and red kangaroos are the giants of this tribe.
The quokka's small rounded ears and short tail, as well
as size, help to distinguish it from the other small wallabies.

*Australia's Wildlife Heritage*, 1975.

The 'quokka' is a paddymelon, a type of small wallaby. Its
name is from the Nyungar language of the Perth–Albany
region, the animal itself existing now in large numbers on
Rottnest and Bald islands and in small communities on the
mainland of south-western Western Australia. 'Paddymelon'
is an anglicisation of the Dharug word, and has a variant form
'pademelon' favoured by the scientific community. But in

popular use 'paddymelon' seems more familiar—we think we can see in the word a 'paddy' and a 'melon'. Despite the fact that it doesn't ultimately make sense, the wallaby having nothing to do with either paddies or melons, we prefer this spelling because in language matters we go for the familiar rather than the obscure.

# (Rr)

## Rafferty's rules

Under the Kennett government's Rafferty's rules system
of planning, it is not easy to answer these questions.
Ministerial discretion and a desperate desire to ensure
toxic waste goes to Labor seats seem to be the over-
arching principles—not fair, clear, understandable
planning laws.

Federal Government Hansard, 30 August 1999.

---

Mr Rafferty was created from an underlying word which must
have sounded rather like the common Irish surname and
which gave rise to this opposition of Rafferty to Queensberry—of mayhem to order. The notion of 'Rafferty's rules'
is dependent on the previous existence of the expression
'Queensberry rules', but it has never applied to boxing or
fighting of any kind but rather to generalised disorder.

As for the underlying word, one suggestion is that it is from the British dialectal word 'rafferty' which is a corruption of 'refractory'. This term for a criminal is now obsolete but it was alive in Dickens' day. A refractory's rules would be the opposite of any orderly and civilised behaviour and would pit the lower class against the upperclass Marquis of Queensberry. Or perhaps it comes from another dialect word 'raffety' meaning 'irregular', which is from 'raff' meaning 'a confused heap or medley'. Certainly that element of confusion is a strong component of 'Rafferty's rules'.

## ratbag

Silence in our society is regarded as consent. The voices of women, made thin by traditional lack of authority and conditioned diffidence, are not breaking the silence, or if they do, women take the chance of being called ratbag troublemakers, man-haters, professional victims and bleaters.

*Advertiser* (Adelaide), 1986.

'Ratbag' derives from the now obsolete expression 'to get a rat' (or 'rats'), meaning to have wild ideas. One aspect of its meaning is straight-out abuse for someone who is a bastard. It can also be a term for someone who is not thought of as doing anything in any way harmful to anyone else, but who is different from others and therefore possibly not to be relied on to have the same reactions and responsibilities as the average person. No substantiated charge—just an intuitive sniffing out of difference. 'He's a bit of a ratbag, but okay for this, that or t'other', you might say. Similarly, ratbaggery is shonkiness at one extreme and simple eccentricity at the other.

**razoo**

OLIVE: Well, go on. What happened?
BARNEY: Nothin'. He went off and I stayed. Then, like I said, I picked him up in Brisbane a week ago. By then he hardly had a razoo.

Ray Lawler, *Summer of the Seventeenth Doll*, 1957.

The 'razoo', brass or otherwise, first appeared in Australian English in World War I as part of the soldiers' slang. No-one knows what the origin of this word is—some suggest Egyptian, others nominate the British Army in India as the source. Another idea is that it is a playful variation on 'sou', as in the expression 'not a sou', which dates back to the late 1700s. Mind you, helpful people have attempted to fill in this gap in our history by creating a coin, usually with inscriptions along the lines of 'the original one-and-only authentic brass razoo'.

## ridge

> Ridge gold, whether in coin or any other shape.
> James Hardy Vaux, *The Flash Language*, 1812.

These days we are more familiar with the variation 'ridgie-didge' (spelled as 'ridgy-didge' or 'ridgey-didge'). This is a colloquialism that ties us to our convict past. Vaux, our convict lexicographer, must have recorded 'ridge' meaning 'gold' around the same time as it became an obsolete term in Britain. As a thieves' term for gold, and then, in particular, a guinea coin, it was used in the 1600s. As an expression of approval it follows a similar path to the word 'gold'. Something, and then someone, vouched for as genuine, is described as 'pure gold' or 'ridge'. The doubling up of the sound in 'ridgie-didge' is a way of adding emphasis.

## ring-in

> By Wednesday morning the thrill of a rout for Hawke was in the air: the executive elections were in progress and news was spreading that there were two Left-Centre tickets, both entitled 'Official Progressive', but one coloured white, the other yellow. The 'Hawke ticket' was white; the yellow ticket was a ring-in.
> Blanche d'Alpuget, *Robert J. Hawke: A Biography*, 1982.

James Hardy Vaux describes 'ringing-in' as follows: '*Ringing the changes*, is a fraud practised by *smashers*, who when they receive good money in change of a guinea, &c., *ring-in* one or more pieces of base with great dexterity and then request the party to change them.'

The expression 'ring the changes' goes back to bellringing, but appears then to have been used figuratively in both lawful and unlawful contexts. In criminal slang it referred to changing bad money for good. There were other instances of ringing-in too. Vaux describes 'ringing castors' as the racket of substituting bad hats for good ones in churches or other public assemblies while the attention of the crowd was elsewhere. A 'castor' was a hat.

In the Australian context the fraudulent activity of ringing-in happened at the racetrack. A 'ring-in' was a horse substituted for another not quite as good. Fine Cotton is one of our most memorable ring-ins. There is also a tradition in two-up of substituting a double-headed or double-tailed coin for a genuine one—this is another Australian ring-in. In general, though, the term is used for someone who is unexpected or who is standing in for someone else.

## rogaining

A new word is being coined in outdoor sporting circles—rogaining. It's used for a new form of marathon orienteering and is thought to be a corruption of a

Scandinavian term for endless suffering.
*Sydney Morning Herald*, 27 August 1979.

This is a competitive sport involving cross-country navigation over long distances and entailing movement by day and by night. It involves teams of two to five members who travel on foot, visiting as many as possible of a set number of checkpoints, all within a twenty-four-hour period. Rogaining was an initiative of the Melbourne University Mountaineering Club, the sport being formalised and promoted in 1976. The people who undertook that task—Rod, Gail and Neil Phillips—coined the word in 1973; 'rogaine' was made up of the first letters of their names.

**rosella**

She was a big woman, and she was fond of bright colours: she looked like a giant rosella in her green and red frock and yellow-striped cardigan.

Hyllus Maris and Sonia Borg, *Women of the Sun*, 1985.

'Budgerigar' is an Aboriginal borrowing, so is 'kookaburra', so you might expect 'rosella' to be one too. But no, 'rosella' is in fact a shortening of 'Rose Hiller', a bird found around Rose Hill near Parramatta in New South Wales, once called the 'Rose Hill parrot'. Rose Hill was the original name for

Parramatta and was used from 1788 to 1791, after which it referred only to the hill on which Government House stood. The application of the name to the parrot followed soon after. The alteration to 'rosella' had taken place by the 1830s with a variant spelling 'roselle', and the generalising of the name to different-coloured birds of the same kind was a natural development.

## rosiner

A stiff drink of spirits of whatever kind is a rosner or rozner or rosiner or roziner. This has been extended to denote any person or thing of excellence.

Sidney J. Baker, *The Australian Language*, 1966.

I thought this word had disappeared from Australian English, at least in the cities, but I heard it on the radio just recently in the sense of a 'stunning performance' and greeted it as an old friend. It comes from 'rosin' or 'resin' which, used on the violin bow, makes it play smoothly and sweetly. From the 1930s it has been applied to any alcoholic drink which, like a rosin, improves the performance of the vocal cords. This is a colloquialism we share with the Irish. In Australian English it has extended its meaning to be a token of praise or admiration. A 'rosiner' (or 'roziner', or 'rozner') is a really good thing.

## rotary hoe

His name could have got among the prospects in an advertising department in the mysterious way that names have of doing such a thing. It was always happening—a circular detailing the merits of So-and-so's combs and cutters; a pamphlet on rotary hoes; an art union brochure.

D'Arcy Niland, *The Shiralee*, 1955.

The name of a successful new invention automatically becomes part of world English no matter where it comes from. The bionic ear may have been named by its inventors in Melbourne, but that is what it is now called throughout the world. In the same way, the 'rotary hoe' went from Cliff Howard's workshop on his Gilgandra farm to general recognition and use. It was an Australian invention that had worldwide application. The prototype was built in 1920 as a series of L-shaped blades on a rotor, the blades set far enough apart to allow the soil to pass through. The secret of its success was that the hoe was free to move over the top of the soil while the blades sliced through the earth, allowing the hoe to move forward when the earth packed in front of the blade, or when there were obstacles like rocks or tree stumps.

## rouseabout

He was the rouseabout, wearing his best clothes with
awful unusualness. The coat was too long in the sleeve,
and wrinkled across the back with his bush slouch.
There was that wonderful margin of loose shirt between
waistcoat and trousers, which all swagger bushies affect.
Subordinate to nothing decorative was the flaring silk
handkerchief, drawn into a sailor's knot round his neck.

Barbara Baynton, 'Billy Skywonkie' in
*Bush Studies*, 1902.

In British dialect 'to rouse about' has a basic meaning 'to stir
up'. It is like our word 'rouse', pronounced 'rowz', meaning
'to disturb or awaken'. Its further meaning is 'to make a great
noise and fuss and generally be busy in a very noisy way'. The
person who made all this noise was then called a 'rouse-about',
and was usually large, loud and able to make their presence
felt. There was also a kind of pea called a 'rouseabout', so
named because it was of a very large size and very round and
'hopped around' more than others.

The first Australian citation is quite late—1861—so it is
not a word that has travelled through military jargon or
convict classifications, and its appearance in the hierarchy of
the shearing shed is not explained. The skilled people in the
shearing shed were the shearers, the fleece-pickers and the
wool-sorters. The 'rouseabouts' had no skills and were
employed to look after the penned sheep, gather up the

fleeces, and generally sweep and tidy and be helpful. Perhaps all these different activities made them seem busier and more bustling than anyone else; perhaps they were yelled at (stirred up or 'roused about') all the time.

Certainly the job developed its own boundaries and status so that it was possible to distinguish between experienced rouseabouts and juniors. It also made the jump from noun to verb. By the late 1800s 'to rouseabout' was an accepted way of earning a living, and not just in the shearing shed. In various places of work such as the farm, the kitchen, the printery, the useful assistant with no particular skills came to be called 'the rouseabout'. Australians are prone to abbreviate occupational titles, so 'rouseabout' became 'rousie' or 'rouser'.

# (Ss)

## sandgroper

When are we Sandgropers going to take the plunge and become a part of this so called national football competition? It's ridiculous that the WA footy public is expected to support the West Coast Eagles in one breath but is deprived of live telecasts of crucial AFL matches.

*West Australian*, 1992.

Rivalries between the states seem to be as strong as ever, but the term 'cabbage gardener' or 'cabbage patcher' for the Victorians seems to have dropped completely out of fashion, as has 'cornstalk' for someone from New South Wales and 'Apple Islander' for a Tasmanian. 'Sandgropers' (West Australians) still abound, as do 'croweaters' (South Australians), 'banana-benders' (Queenslanders) and 'top-enders' (Territorians).

Because New South Wales was the first state, there was a brief period of time in the 1880s when 'Cornstalk' was the equivalent of 'Australian', with visitors to the colony commenting on how tall and slender were the currency lads and lasses, that is, the children born in Australia.

## screamer

Sailors make lousy lovers because they suffer a four week build-up for a one-minute screamer, women have found. A long, regular relationship creates more satisfying sex, they say.

*News* (Adelaide), 3 July 1990.

To understand 'screamer' as a noun we need to look at the verb 'to scream' which has as a base meaning 'to travel at great speed while making a loud noise', as in 'The rocket screamed overhead'. In Australian English the focus is less on the noise than on the speed. Someone who takes a high mark in Aussie Rules is, therefore, said to have pulled down a screamer. An unusually large wave travelling at great speed is also a screamer. A further development of the meaning concentrates solely on the exceptional size, strength or brilliance of the thing described, so anything spectacular can be referred to as a 'screamer'.

## scrub

> After they had walked for a couple of hours, sometimes leaving the river and cutting through the scrub and the blackwood trees, Bunjil motioned them to stop and rest.
> Michael Hyde, *Will You Shut Up about Spiritmen!*, 1982.

'Scrub' is related to 'shrub' and means a low, stunted bush. In British English 'scrub' would be land covered with low bushes. In Australian and New Zealand English the bushes are bigger although they are still straggly and untidy rather than well-formed and shapely trees, and can be quite impenetrable. From a type of vegetation the word extends in meaning to refer to the tract of land covered with this vegetation. And, just as we have 'bush' and 'the Bush', so too we have 'scrub' and 'the Scrub', to mean the remote parts of Australia and the people who live there.

## shanghai

> She was a bit of a tomboy. But I suppose with four brothers and no sisters, she had to be. She could do most things we did. She was a good shot with a rifle and not bad with a shanghai.
> Barney Roberts, *Where's Morning Gone?*, 1987.

Received wisdom on 'shanghai' was that it related to the practices on the Shanghai waterfront in the 1870s where a vessel would obtain its crew by drugging and carting off unfortunate men who wandered past.

The image here is of something heading in one direction and then being swiftly sent off in the opposite direction. This produced the verb to describe, for example, how an animal forcing its way through the scrub would be 'shanghaied' backwards by the springy saplings. The catapult or shanghai produces the same swift reversal of direction. The stone moves back against the strain of the thong and then flies off with the recoil.

An alternative origin is from the Scottish dialect word 'shangie', originally referring to a stick cleft at one end so that it could be attached to a dog's tail. Different times, different amusements. This etymology is linked to the shape of the catapult, the other to the movement of the catapulted object.

### shanty

After a few miles on the new track, a blob glittered dazzlingly through the glare, like a fallen star. It was the iron roof of the wine shanty—the Saturday night and Sunday resort of shearers and rouseabouts for twenty miles around. Most of its spirits was made on the premises from bush recipes, of which bluestone and tobacco were the chief ingredients.

Barbara Baynton, 'Billy Skywonkie' in
*Bush Studies*, 1902.

A 'shanty' in colonial Australian English was an establishment to sell liquor. Mostly it was a hut or tent in the bush somewhere and, more often than not, was unlicensed. The origin of this word lies in the French 'chantier', a worksite or depot. Canadian French extended that meaning in the context of the timber industry to refer to the small hut which served as the headquarters of the logging site—inevitably a fairly rough and ready building put together from scraps of timber. From there, 'shanty' makes the leap into the Australian colony, probably via the goldrush since the earliest citation is in the 1860s.

Other terms for the illegal public house were 'sly-grog shop', which is self-evident, and 'shypoo shop', which is of unknown origin.

### sheila

'Den's been me mate for a long time. Up to now, he's always managed to keep out of trouble. He's had hundreds o' sheilas in 'is time, but none of 'em ever hooked 'im permanent. So don't count on this one...'
Nino Culotta, *Gone Fishin'*, 1962.

'Sheila' was a common female name in Ireland, used alongside the name 'Paddy' to represent the archetypal Irish couple.

From this early usage (dating from the 1820s in Britain) 'sheila' came to mean any female, whether Irish or not. This British use of 'sheila' was then transported to the colonies. In Australian English, however, the 'sheila' is partnered by a 'bloke' rather than a 'Paddy'. While blokes and sheilas can still be found in outback Australia, in our urban habitats they have been replaced by the unisex 'guys'.


## shepherd

> I shepherded that girl, sir
> And soon got in such a flame
> That I fancied every fellow there
> Was going to jump my claim.
> William W. Coxon(?), 'The German Girls' in *Coxon's Comic Songster*, c. 1850s.

Before the goldrush in Australia 'shepherding' had to do with looking after sheep. The influx of miners in the 1850s brought about many changes in Australian English where old words acquired new meanings. Shepherding came to mean looking after a potential mine. It was often the case that although miners might suspect that gold was to be found further on from where they were working, they didn't have the resources to investigate it immediately. So they sent one of their group to turn over a spadeful of dirt each day just to show that this was an active claim. This was called 'shepherding the claim'.

The quote above shows the further use of 'shepherd' when the 'claim' was a person rather than a patch of dirt. This extension of the metaphor is the basis for our modern use of the word which implies watchful surveillance and responsible care.

A further use is in Aussie Rules for that manoeuvre in which one player blocks the path of the opposition to give a team member room to move.

## shivoo

> Then Tim said to Cedric, 'Yeah—there's gonner be a weddin' at Black Adder Creek. The first. Who'd've thought it a week ago! We'll make a bonzer shivoo of it too. Booze—dancin'—all the people in the country there…'
>
> Xavier Herbert, *Capricornia*, 1938.

It would seem to be a reasonable guess that 'shivoo' is derived from 'chez vous', meaning 'at your place', perhaps part of a response to a party invitation. But some are not so sure. In British English, the first citation is dated 1798 and the form of the word is 'chevaux'. Other forms are 'chiveau', 'shebo' and 'sheevo', although the most common form is 'shiveau'. This, in Australian English, becomes 'shivoo'.

## shonky

> These are not backdated contracts, they are not shonky
> contracts, they are not 'nudge, nudge, wink, wink'
> contracts; they are serious contracts that were signed.
>
> Federal Government Hansard, 21 October 1999.

British slang of the early 1900s produced 'shonk' as an offensive name for a Jew, taken from the Yiddish *shonnicker* meaning 'trader' or 'peddler'. This, with the addition of the diminutive '-ie', became 'shonkie' meaning 'a tightfisted person'.

All of this still seems a long way from the Australian use of the word dating from the 1970s to mean 'not quite right, not authentic, not quite honest'. A shonky car was sold in the knowledge that it was not operating properly. A shonky deal was a dishonest one.

But does it relate to the British 'shonkie'? G. A. Wilkes suggests in *A Dictionary of Australian Colloquialisms* that the Australian 'shonky' is our own invention and simply a blend of 'shoddy' and 'wonky'.

## shout

> Bill the donkey-driver had come to town and was
> shouting drinks for the crowd.
>
> Thomas Wood, *Cobbers*, 1934.

This Australian practice of treating one's friends to a round of drinks originated in old-style pubs and taverns of the 1800s where the noise level demanded that to be served you had to raise your voice. The person who 'shouted' the order to the bar put together the collective order, and paid for it. It was easier and more sociable to offer to shout and pay for the next round rather than work out who owed what to whom on each order. This system transferred to many contexts in which raising one's voice was no longer an issue so the meaning of the word 'shout' focused on the notion of treating one's companions.

## skerrick

What would we use for wood?
Yeah, that's right. Not even a bloody skerrick of wood about.
A pair of green swagmen, they were.
D'Arcy Niland, *The Shiralee*, 1955.

The word 'skerrick' is a hand-me-down from dialects of northern English, and usually appeared in the negative—'I don't care a skerrick' or 'I don't give a skerrick'. These are constructions in which we have been known to use such benchmarks of our apathy as 'brass razoo', 'tinker's cuss', 'a twopenny dump', and more recently 'a damn', 'a toss', 'a monkey's', 'a rat's arse' and, not surprisingly, 'a shit'.

In Australian English, 'skerrick' means 'a tiny bit'. A related form in British dialect is 'skuddick' which is from 'skud' meaning a twist of straw. This could be the origin, but no one knows for sure.

## skite

> EMMA: Why do you think Barney lied about your back?
> ROO: Lyin' comes as natural to him as skiting.
> EMMA: Not always, it didn't. You listen—before Barney started to get the brush-off from women, he only skited. Now he lies.
>
> Ray Lawler, *Summer of the Seventeenth Doll*, 1957.

One thing the average Australian cannot stand is the 'skite', a person who continually tells the world at large how wonderful they are. The word is a shortened form of the Scottish word 'bletherskate' for a person who talks too much.

'Blether', with its variants 'blither' and 'blather' comes from an Old Norse word meaning 'to talk nonsense'. 'Skate' developed from a Scottish word for 'a sudden movement or slip', and from there to 'a trick', and so to 'a trickster'. The bletherskate's purpose was to deceive you and the wary took anything they said with a large grain of salt.

In Australian English the skite talks up their achievements, real or, as the audience rightly suspects, somewhat exaggerated, rather than letting their deeds speak for themselves.

## slouch hat

> I was wearing my slouch hat, with its rising sun badge
> on the turned up side, and I had my hands in my
> pockets. 'Well, Mick,' said Eddie as we neared the
> artillery lines, 'How's it feel? Ya feel like a solider?'
> 'Soldier? No. I feel as if I'm going to a fancy dress ball.'
> Lawson Glassop, *We Were the Rats*, 1944.

The slouch hat has, for Australians, become the symbol of
the soldier, representing the courage and patriotism
shown by those who went to war. It dates back to the 1880s
in Australia and was adopted, it is said, by Colonel Tom
Price when he enlisted volunteers for the Victorian
Mounted Rifles. The soldiers turned the brim up on the
right side to avoid catching it during rifle drill. Since
the Boer War, however, it has been turned up on the
left.

But why does the hat 'slouch'? In the late 1700s, Britons
on the wrong side of the law slouched their hats to conceal
their faces. A very early meaning of 'slouch' was to hang down
or droop, so 'to slouch your hat' was to pull the brim down so
that it hung over your face. By the 1800s a slouch hat was a
hat of soft or unstiffened felt with a broad brim dropping over
the face. In the Australian context the most recognised form
of the slouch hat is now the akubra.

## smoodge

> He'd go round to the kitchen for a hand-out, and if
> there was no blokes about, he'd come the smoodge to
> the women for a bit of a love-up.
>
> D'Arcy Niland, *The Shiralee*, 1955.

'Smoodging' is basically kissing and cuddling. It comes from British dialect, particularly from northern dialects like Yorkshire. In Australian English of the early 1900s it developed the meaning 'to flatter'. To 'do the smoodge' is to ingratiate yourself with someone, and a 'smoodger' is a sycophantic person.

This negative meaning seems less common now, although the smoodging in the backseat of the car is still an option.

## sook

> Alan had tears in his eyes. The teacher watched him
> walk away and thought, hating himself for it: cry-baby,
> sook, bellowing big calf of a boy.
>
> Garry Disher, 'The Bamboo Flute' in *Bundle of Yarns*,
> 1986.

'Sook' is the pronunciation of the word 'suck' which has a cluster of meanings common throughout dialects of Scotland, England and Ireland. The basic notion of sucking at the breast gives rise to a number of meanings and combinations of the word. 'Suck-a-buss' means an overgrown child that still wants the breast. In Scottish dialect a 'sook' was a term for a stupid person, someone who sucked at the breast too long. A 'sookie' was a suckling but then also a term for a petted or over-indulged child. It is clear that, beyond a certain age, the urge to run home to mother is one that earns general contempt.

In Australian English 'sook' is still an operative term of abuse among children and, in a milder form, from adults who wish to remind their children that they ought to grow up.

## sool

Bluey howled and plunged until Mother came out to see what was the matter. She was in time to see a solitary kangaroo hop in a drunken manner towards the fence, so she let the dog go and cried, 'Sool him, Bluey! Sool him!' Bluey sooled him, and Mother followed with the axe to get the scalp.

Steele Rudd, *On Our Selection*, 1899.

To 'sool a dog on' is to incite it to worry or harass another animal, and as a command to a dog, 'Sool 'im!' still has currency. It has, however, had other meanings in Australian English which seem to have dropped out of use.

A 'sooler' was the equivalent of an urger—someone who eventually persuades someone to do something. To 'sool someone on' was to urge them to do something that they would probably later regret. In both world wars there were factions that were strident in urging others on to fight while staying at home themselves. In 1936 a Sydney publication called the *Publicist* commented, 'Women instinctively sool on the soldiery as soon as a war begins.'

'Sool' has developed yet another meaning—'to run away' or 'scarper'. 'To sool along' is to travel at a fast pace and 'to sool off' is to disappear at speed. These uses of 'sool' do not seem to have much currency these days. Sport provides examples of the current use: 'a jockey sools his mount on' and 'Geelong claws, scratches and sools its way back into the match'.

'Sool' is from British dialect 'sowl' meaning 'to pull by the ears'. Shakespeare was familiar with it as the following quote from *Coriolanus* Act IV scene v shows: 'He'll go, he says, and sowl the porter of Rome gates by the ears.'

### spieler

A speler is known as a man that can do without working, and who travels from meeting to meeting with a pack of cards or a dice box in his hand. To offer him work would be to take a liberty quite unwarranted. They are independent men; they have no need to work; they live by their wits, and I dare say they make a good living at their calling.

*Adelaide Observer*, 29 May 1886.

The *Observer* may have felt the necessity to explain this new word to its readers because it had come from American English—from the German 'spieler' meaning 'to gamble'—and had appeared in Sydney roughly a decade before. The most common meaning of 'spieler' nowadays is 'glib talker', from the verb 'to spiel' meaning to perform a verbal patter, especially one designed to advertise or deceive. 'Spieling' is another word for swindling, particularly in the form of card-sharping. A 'spiel' has survived as a mild put-down for a longwinded speech or explanation.

### squatter

A 'squatter' is a freed, or 'ticket of leave' man, who builds a hut with bark on unoccupied ground, buys or steals a few animals, sells spirits without a licence, receives stolen goods—and so at last becomes rich and turns farmer: he is the horror of his honest neighbours.

Charles Darwin, *Report to the Select Committee on Transportation*, 1837.

In its earliest use 'squatter', a borrowing from American English, referred to someone who squatted on land, that is, seized it unofficially for their own use. The squatter in Australia, however, was often able to occupy vast amounts of land and become extremely rich. The word moved upmarket along with

squatter

the person it designated, so that in 1843 the *Melbourne Times* could refer to 'gentleman settlers, designated squatters'.

The squatter was very different from the 'free selector' who took up the opportunity offered by the government to buy a small parcel of land. The terms were generally favourable but the parcel of land, or 'selection' as it was called, was small, so selectors as a group struggled and were akin to the 'cocky farmer'.

## station

> The life of a soldier on a convict station was a hard one. He was often stinted in rations, and of necessity deprived of all rational recreation, while punishment for offences was prompt and severe.
>
> Marcus Clarke, *For the Term of His Natural Life*, 1874.

The special Australian use of 'station' for a rural property comes from its military use for an outpost of a colonial government, a place where troops are stationed for a particular purpose. In the early days of settlement that purpose was to superintend the work of convicts, which gave rise to the term 'convict station'. A very remote location was called an 'outstation'. This military use was adopted in church use as in 'mission station', and in agricultural use as in 'cattle station' and 'sheep station'. If you had permission to occupy a tract of grazing land, then you had 'right of station'. The 'station' also came to mean the 'home station' or the chief building and headquarters of a station, and in this sense it gave rise to a number of compounds—'station boss', 'station cook', 'station horse', 'station house', 'station yard'.

## stinging tree

The traditional recipe for Banyan Rum was very simple. 'Two gallons of overproof rum, a pound of salt to keep you drinking, two tablespoons of water, an armful of leaves off a stinging tree and a pound plug of tobacco nailed to the bottom of the keg. Allow to mature for five minutes. If you're a fussy bastard you can strain it through a greasy horse blanket.'

Wendy Lowenstein and Morag Loh,
*The Immigrants*, 1977.

The 'stinging tree' is the colloquial term for the tree more formally identified as the 'gympie'. This is not a tree that you would welcome into your garden; it has huge leaves, the size of dinner plates, which are hairy with transparent, stinging spines. Its fruit is covered in spines also. Apparently it is impossible to remove them and they can cause an ache for days after contact. The tree belongs to the nettle family Urticaceae, and grows to a height of five metres.

'Gympie' occurs in a number of Aboriginal languages of the region. As is often the case in these languages, it was reduplicated as 'gympie gympie' but in Australian English we have settled for the single-word version.

The Queensland town of Gympie is named after the plant. It was originally a mining town called Nashville which grew out of the discovery of gold by James Nash in 1867. Its name was changed just one year later to honour the local nettle.

## stone the crows

At last McBee lowered the paper. 'Stone the crows'—rural terms had penetrated the urban vocabulary in South Australia, along with mining slang—'anyone would think I was bringing Jane Russell into the house.'

Murray Bail, *Holden's Performance*, 1988.

Inventiveness in language can be found in the exclamations of joy, surprise or anger that we make. The content doesn't matter much given that the meaning in context is obvious. 'Stone the crows' is an expression that belongs to this category and although regarded as particularly Australian, there is a suggestion that we may have acquired it from Cockney. It seems to have been acquired from World War I, initially appearing as 'starve the crows' or 'stiffen the crows'. By the 1920s it had settled into the current idiom.

## strike me dead!

> And we each said in turn, to the dozen or so men in the
> coach, 'Well, thanks, gentlemen. Good morning', or
> something like that. The only reply reached my ears
> when, I like to think, we were considered out of earshot.
> It was simply: 'Gawd strike me dead.'
>
> Harold Lewis, *Crow on a Barbed Wire Fence*, 1973.

A catchphrase is an expression by which we convey our
mood—happiness, sadness, anger and frustration, whimsicality or resignation. Such idioms are more vulnerable to fashion
than other elements of our language and so become indica-
tors of a particular time or place.

The phrase 'strike me lucky', which 'strike me dead'
echoes, is not actually an Australian invention, despite its
strong association with the comedian Roy Rene in his character Mo. It was part of British English before Mo gave it such
a high profile, although we did play around with the idea in
ways that are unique to us. The cry could just as easily have
been 'strike me dead' or 'fat' or 'handsome', or 'strike me
blue', 'pink', or 'roan'.

In essence, the call to be 'struck' in some specified way is
a jocular invocation to the gods to transform the speaker into
something unpleasant—or at least embarrassing—'pink' or
'blue' or 'fat'. Being struck 'handsome' is I think a joke, as is
being struck 'lucky'—a wish to hoodwink God into doing
something he didn't intend.

## Strine

> Dr Mahathir said Chinese in Australia were forced to use the local language leading to the unusual Australian accent.
>
> 'The rain in Spain falls mainly in the plain, the rain in Spain falls mainly in the plain', he said with an Australian strine, ABC television reported.
>
> AAP News Service, 24 June 2001.

It was no doubt hard to capture in a newspaper report Dr Mahathir's send-up of the Australian accent but it was a curious little venture into language stereotyping. The term 'Strine' was the invention of Alistair Ardoch Morrison, a *Sydney Morning Herald* artist and graphic designer in the 1960s. The idea came about from a report of a book launch in which a British author asked a book-buyer queuing for an autographed copy for their name. 'Emma chisit?' said the would-be purchaser, and so the author duly wrote Emma Chisit in the book, not realising that this was Strine for 'How much is it?'

'Strine' itself is a Strine pronunciation of 'Australian'. Morrison published *Let Stalk Strine* in 1965 under the pseudonym of Afferbeck Lauder. The book is an exaggerated representation of the broad Australian accent of a small proportion of the community. It focuses on the elisions and distortions of words that commonly happen in speech but seem absurd when written down. It is extraordinary that a book with such limited scope should have produced such a key term for Australians.

## stump-jump plough

> Cattle browsed in paddocks eaten out of the bush by fire and axe, cleared with stump-jump plough, and fenced with posts and rails.
>
> Thomas Wood, *Cobbers*, 1934.

The 'stump-jump plough' was designed to overcome the difficulty of ploughing partially cleared ground. It was no easy task to remove the stumps, particularly when they were mallee stumps and hard as rocks. The idea behind this new plough was that the ploughshare which cuts or turns the soil hung loosely, suspended on the frame by a single bolt to give it sufficient freedom of movement to be able to ride over the stumps. The share is brought back into alignment by a weight on the end of a lever which forces it back into the soil.

The invention is credited to Robert Bowyer Smith, a farmer from Kalkabury in the mallee country of South Australia. The story goes that as he ploughed his land with a fixed ploughshare one of the bolts broke on the stumpy ground. Rather than fix the plough he decided to carry on with the ploughshare hanging loose and, to his surprise, found that it worked much better. The first version was completed in 1876 and by the 1880s was acclaimed as the second-greatest gift to farmers after the stripper for harvesting wheat.

## sundowner

> For superior city-persons looking through the window, the sight of a dusty figure carrying its swag along the road beside the railway line was enough evidence for the mental classification: 'Genus—tramp; species—something of the sort that pokes its head over suburban back fences; sundowner, swaggie, unemployed.'
>
> C. E. W. Bean, *On the Wool Track*, 1910.

A 'sundowner' timed his arrival at the homestead too late to do any actual work, and too late for it to be reasonable to send him on his way elsewhere. It would become the inevitable responsibility of the station owner to provide him with some supplies and maybe even some accommodation.

Another term for the lifestyle of the sundowner was 'tea-and-sugar burgling' or 'tea-and-sugar bushranging', those two commodities being essential requirements along the track.

## swag

> Battling with poverty, footsore and sad,
> Things only look middling with me.
> Some shearing I found to my great surprise,

The price being five bob a score:
I threw down my swag, saying 'Dash my old rags
If I ever hump you any more.'
    Anon, 'The Poor Bushman' in *Old Bush Recitations*,
                   1932.

---

In British dialects, particularly in the north, there is an expression 'to swag' which means 'sway from side to side'. There is the notion behind it that the swaying is caused by the weight of a burden, so an overladen cart is said to swag, or a person carrying a large and heavy bundle. From this there developed a sense of the noun 'swag' meaning a burden of some kind, possibly the contents of your wallet or pocket, possibly the basket of goods that a pedlar would carry, or, in thieves' talk, the booty that you carried away from a robbery. In the context of colonial life the 'swag' became the bundle of belongings that the swagman carried or 'humped' on his back as he walked from place to place.

# (Tt)

## tall poppy syndrome

> While the tall poppy syndrome continues to reign in Australia, players like Norman will take a hammering from those who choose to dig out the worst when an athlete goes through a bad patch...Ironically, as I was pounding out these words, a colleague walked by and noticed a copy of *Golf Australia* on my desk which boasted a picture of Norman on the front cover, and he simply remarked: 'Norman the Great White Dork'.
>
> *Mercury* (Hobart), 1992.

The 'tall poppy syndrome' refers to the way in which people make gratuitous attacks on those known for their excellence in a particular field. The idiom is supposed to have derived from a folk story about Tarquin the Proud, the last king of

Rome. Tarquin's son, Sesto, had managed to ingratiate himself with the citizens of Gabii, a town that Tarquin wanted to conquer. Tarquin wanted to send Sesto a message to the effect that he should start killing the most important citizens of Gabii, but who do you trust with such a message? He resolved the difficulty by pruning the tallest poppies in the garden before the messenger's puzzled gaze. In the absence of anything more meaningful, the messenger reported the fact to Sesto who understood instantly what he must do.

The first recorded mention of tall poppies is, however, in the context of the wheat field where the poppies are growing taller than the young wheat and need to be cut back. This is dated 1641. The first Australian quotation comes from the New South Wales Parliamentary Debates of 1931 where the premier of the day is attacking a privileged class which he describes as 'tall poppies'.

### terra nullius

Despite his professed admiration for the New Hollanders, Cook took their lands as if they did not exist; they became from that moment a shadow people with no rights of any kind to their hearths and homes. This was an application of the dictum of terra nullius (land without people); following it no restrictions were recognised on occupation or exploitation.

Al Grassby and Marji Hill, *Six Australian Battlefields*,
1988.

This is a legal term introduced into popular consciousness by
first the Mabo case in 1992 and then Wik in 1996. It is a term
that goes back to Roman law when scholars argued the legal-
ities of the expansion of the empire. The simplest case was the
deserted island that 'belonged to no-one'. Whoever found
uninhabited land first could claim it. European law, based on
Roman law, attempted to modify this concept and to redefine
'inhabited' to include 'demonstrating a regulated system of
property ownership'. If you stumbled on an island that wasn't
ordered in this way then you could claim it. The extended
concept of terra nullius always had a dubious status in
European law.

British law operated according to different principles. If
you found unoccupied land you could claim it. If there were
people there you could conquer them or bargain with them.
It was never entirely clear what category the colonists put the
Aborigines in, but certainly it was central to the Mabo case
that the European settlers had dismissed the Aborigines as not
having the systems of the civilised world in terms of law and
property ownership, and thus claimed the land. Mabo
reasserted that the Aborigines did exist, had prior ownership
and still had rights that needed to be addressed. The phrase
'terra nullius' sums up the colonial view even though it was
not used at that time.

## tombowler

> Who stole my marble holder?
> Tombowlers, blood reels and cats eyes: Things kept in
> an alley bag.
>
> Phillip Adams, *The Unspeakable Adams*, 1974.

---

A tombowler is a large marble, about twice the diameter of an ordinary marble. The alternative spelling is 'tombola' which is from an Italian word meaning 'tumble' and is also the name of a popular game of chance. An alternative explanation is that 'tom' means 'large', since males of many animals are larger than the females, and 'bowler' is a ball that bowls along. Australian kids have been quite eloquent and inventive in naming the various marbles they have played with over the years. Here is a brief list: 'aggies' or 'agates' were highly prized marbles, made from real quartz; an even rarer sort was the 'connie agate'. An 'alley' was a largish marble, possibly so-named because they were once made of alabaster; a 'blood alley' was a red one. A 'bottler' or 'bottley' or 'glassy' was a clear glass stopper from an early type of soft-drink bottle. Any glass marble, even a coloured one, can be called a 'glassie' and is distinguished from a 'china' (nowadays usually white-coloured glass). Metal ball bearings used as marbles are called 'steelies' or 'steelos'. Marbles named after their colourings include 'cat's eye', 'lorikeet' (red and yellow), 'peewee' (black and white) and 'slatey' (grey). A large marble was sometimes called a 'bonker', 'bully' or 'stonker'. Marbles in general were known as 'dakes', 'dibs', 'doogs', 'dooks' or 'taws'. Some of these names are very old—'alley', short for alabaster, dates back to the eighteenth century. Others, like 'steelie', are quite new.

## tommy rough

Fish averaged 7 to 9kg and dusk appears to be the best time, using garfish or tommy ruff for bait.

*Mail* (Adelaide), 1989.

The most common spelling for this fish, 'tommy rough', illustrates the way in which we turn words into familiar spellings at the expense of fact and meaning. The European settlers gave the name 'ruff' to a fish like the one they knew back home. That original fish may well have been rough but that's just a guess. Certainly there is a freshwater fish of the perch family in England that had prickly scales. But our 'ruff' is not rough. Its official name is 'Australian herring', also a misleading name because it belongs to the Australian salmon or sea perch family.

The name 'Tom' had the diminutive 'Tommy' which in British English was applied to all sorts of things to indicate that they were small versions of their kind. For example, a 'tommy bar' was a small metal bar. It is not a naming practice that has currency in Australian English but it survives in the name 'tommy rough'.

## toodlembuck

In the weeks before the Melbourne Cup was run
we gambled with cherry bobs (cherry stones) on a
toodlembuck. This was a small whirligig of cardboard
with the Cup horses' names printed round the edge.
The spring racing season caused a peak demand for
cherry bobs.

Ross Campbell, *The Road to Oxalis Cottage*, 1981.

It is hard to describe a 'toodlembuck' to those who have never
seen one. It is a device used in a gambling game for children
and made from a disc of stiff cardboard glued onto a cotton
reel which spins on a meat skewer. The 'toodlembuck' is made
to spin by winding a string around the cotton reel and then
pulling it sharply. The top of the skewer is split to hold a
pointer to indicate the winner from a series of options listed
in sections on the piece of cardboard. Childish bookmakers
used to have childish bagmen with bags full of cherrybobs
(cherry stones) for money.

## true believer

The sound bite should have been more humble.
Instead, only the opening line was remembered, and for
much of the next three years we would battle the
perception that the words meant his victory had only

been for the faithful and the rest of the country could go hang. Later it was hard not to think that just as they were going to put the axe back in the woodheap the people of Australia heard him say on television, 'This is a victory for the true believers,' and they decided to leave it at the back door ready for next time.

Don Watson, *Recollections of a Bleeding Heart*, 2002.

'True Believer' had its beginnings in evangelical regions of the US. Its crossover into politics came with Eric Hoffer (1902–83) who, in 1951, wrote a book called *The True Believer: Thoughts on the Nature of Mass Movements*. In it he described the working-class person who puts his faith in a large, somehow ennobling movement which gives him something to hope for. The expression is used with affection by one true believer to another, and as a sneer by its detractors. In Australia it has been adopted and is used to identify ideologues of the Australian Labor Party.

**true-blue**

Perhaps the most obvious evidence of the trend will be seen in its influence on TV advertising in the 90s. Out will go the overworked true blue Aussie and other nationalistic themes.

*Advertiser* (Adelaide), 1 May 1990.

The history of some of our most cherished words and phrases lies often in British English or British dialect. We do, nevertheless, lay claim to items that we feel mean more to us than they do to speakers of other Englishes. What is an Aussie but 'dinky-di' and 'true-blue'? The colour 'blue' as a symbol for constancy dates back to medieval times and the actual expression came to us from British English where it either meant 'totally loyal' or, in the 1800s, 'a committed member of the Conservative Party'. For us the 'true-blue Aussie' is, as this quote suggests, an icon that belongs to an earlier time.


## trugo

> Trugo has a following of more than 400 players...The disc (plastic these days) is placed between the feet, the back is turned to the opposite end of the rink and the disc is hit 28 metres—hopefully between the posts which are almost two metres apart.
>
> *Sunday Press* (Melbourne), 2 December 1979.

Trugo is an Australian contribution to the world of sport. It began with a group of workers at the Newport railway yards in Melbourne in the 1920s who, casting around for something to do to amuse themselves in their lunchbreak, decided that it would be a fine idea to try to hit some of the rubber wheels they had around them between an improvised goal. The wheel was to be hit with a mallet from far enough away to make it difficult. One of them scored a hit between the posts to which another contestant responded 'That was a true go!' in the sense of a true aim. And so the game became known as 'trugo'. The alternative explanation is that 'trugo' comes from the name of the 'father' of the sport, Thomas Greaves. Both stories sound a bit contrived and I have never found either of these explanations for the name convincing. The rules have now been established and the game apparently has a devoted although small following among Melbourne retirees. The method described above is called 'tunnelling' and is preferred by men. Women tend to favour 'side-swiping' which is similar to the action used in croquet.


**tucker**

> She was not afraid of horsemen: but swagmen, going to, or worse, coming from the dismal, drunken little township, a day's journey beyond, terrified her. One had called at the house today, and asked for tucker.
>
> Barbara Baynton, 'The Chosen Vessel' in *Bush Studies*, 1902.

In British slang of the late 1700s 'to tuck something away', meaning to consume it, was a schoolboy witticism. From that starting point came 'tuck into' meaning 'to begin to eat heartily' and 'tucker', being whatever it was that was tucked away. All from that original image of your stomach as some kind of capacious pocket into which you folded your food and drink. In the Australian context the joke had already faded and 'tucker' was simply supplies of food and drink. The 'tucker box' or 'bag' was the container in which you carried provisions. The expression 'make tucker' meant 'to earn a subsistence living'. These days 'tucker' survives in slightly jokey remarks about something being 'good tucker', or else in the term 'bush tucker' and other collocations equivalent to cuisine, as with 'Greek tucker', 'Indonesian tucker', etc.

The expression 'tuckered out' has nothing to do with the consumption of tucker. It is an Americanism that we adopted in the early 1900s. The origin is not clear but one suggestion is that it relates to the British dialectal expressions 'tucked up' and 'twickered out', both meaning 'exhausted'.

## two-bob

> The 1950s in Australia were years of rawness and unsophistication…where European migrants were referred to as 'Bloody Balts' or 'Dagos' and their children began to learn about the English language from the distillation of phrases such as 'mad as a two-bob watch' and 'yer silly galah!'.
>
> Peter Skrzynecki, *Joseph's Coat*, 1985.

In former times 'two bob' was two shillings (a 'bob' was a shilling). The coin worth two bob was called a 'florin'. This coin was almost identical in size to the modern twenty-cent piece, brought in with the changeover to decimal currency in 1966, and sometimes still known as 'two bob'. Something worth two-bob was pretty cheap, and so something that 'went like a two-bob watch' didn't work at all well. People could be accused of being 'as silly' or 'as mad as a two-bob watch'— which meant that they were as 'nutty as a fruitcake' or 'mad as a meat axe'. Then there was the 'two-bob lair'—a flashy and ostentatious person who 'put on the dog'. A 'two-bob boss' was a petty official, who threw his weight about in a highly officious manner. A 'two-bob millionaire' was someone who paraded their new-found wealth. To 'have two-bob each way' on something is to hedge your bets, to organise things so that no matter what the outcome all will be well. Finally, inexpert or slapdash wielders of the hammer often strike wide of the mark and leave ugly circular indentations in the wood surface. From their shape and size these are called 'two bobs'.


### two-pot screamer

> Ireland displays deep compassion for the industrial working men—Knuckles, Sumpoil, the Two Pot Screamer.
>
> Miriam Dixson, *The Real Matilda*, 1984.

The etiquette of drinking insists that you make allowances for the 'two-pot screamer', largely because they become garrulously drunk at a point when everyone else is still sober enough to find them amusing. They are often people whose physiological and psychological make-up conspires to make them curiously susceptible to alcohol. This means that they light up like firecrackers at a gathering only to fizzle out before the party really begins. This 1950s expression 'two-pot screamer' can also be a 'two-schooner screamer' or a 'two-middy screamer' depending on local custom.

## two-up

Grant, like every Australian, had heard of Two-Up Schools. Every city has one and in the outback, miners, labourers, railwaymen, anybody desperate for diversion—and that is almost everybody—will gather from a radius of a hundred miles to wager on the fall of the illegal pennies.

Kenneth Cook, *Wake in Fright*, 1961.

There are references to 'two-up' in the very early days of the colony, when it was known as 'chuck-farthing', as it was called in Britain. The first reference to 'chuck-farthing' dates back to the 1600s, but the term 'two-up' seems to be an Australian innovation which appears in the late 1800s.

At the moment when the boxer—the man in charge of the ring—has decided that all bets have been taken, he will call for the attention of the onlookers so that the spinner can toss the coins. 'Fair go, spinner,' he'll say, meaning 'Give the spinner a fair go'. The name 'two-up' comes from the fact that this national institution is based on the toss of two coins. It is also called a 'swy game'—'swy' being a corruption of the German word 'zwei', meaning 'two'.

There is a cluster of words associated with 'two-up'. First is the notion of the 'two-up school' or group involved in a game which was often run in an alley. The person running the game is the 'ringie' or 'ringkeeper' and the one who tosses the coins is the 'spinner'. The 'centre' holds the bets made by the 'spinner' and the 'alley clerk' arranges bets for a player. A 'headie' backs 'heads', a 'tailie' backs 'tails'. Finally, there is the 'cockatoo' or 'nit-keeper' who keeps watch for the police.

# (Uu)

## uey

…to 'do a uey in a ute at the uni' really means making
a U-turn in a utility truck at the university.
*National Geographic*, February 1979.

The Australian penchant for shortening words and adding the
suffix '-ey' to the end is perhaps brought to perfection in this
word—just a single letter plus the suffix. What makes this
possible, of course, is the fact that the base word 'U-turn'
actually has the single letter as its first syllable.

This extremity in brevity is only matched by one other
term—the 'R-ie', a familiar term for the local RSL Club, also
known as the 'Rissole' or the 'Rozzer'.

## ugari

They searched for ugaries with their toes and found a star
shell and a Chinamen's hat and a reddish brown shark's

egg, a shattered pomegranate, with a split in its leathery covering through which a sharkling had been born.
Ronald McKie, *The Mango Tree*, 1975.

The ugari is a bivalve mollusc common on the Australian coastline. Its name is from the Yagara language spoken in the Moreton Bay district. Several versions of this appeared in English before consensus was reached on 'ugari', other variants being 'eugari' and 'yugari'.

The same shellfish is called 'pipi' in New South Wales, the name being a New Zealand import borrowed in that country from the Maoris who used it to refer to a slightly different mollusc. In Australia this name belongs to a set of regional names—in addition to 'pipi' and 'ugari', we have 'clam' in Tasmania and 'Coorong cockle' or 'Goolwa cockle' in South Australia.

**unco**

Unco: Not with it. 'As if you would wear that brightly coloured dress to a funeral, you're so unco,' said Emily to her friend.
*KiD* (Kids Internet Dictionary), 1995.

'Uncoordinated' is one of those teacherly or parental words aimed at children. Children respond by shortening it to 'unco'—for clumsy actions, garish clothes or generally antisocial behaviour. This shortening to 'unco' is neat because it fits in to the common Australian pattern of adding the suffix '-o' to words such as garbo, journo, etc.

## unity ticket

Similarly, Schools Minister David Kemp is running a popular theme with his crusade on school literacy. Yet his grip on the moral high ground seems a little precarious in the face of an unprecedented unity ticket among state education ministers, teachers and parent bodies.
AAP News Service, 19 September 1997.

In trade union elections of the 1950s, the 'unity ticket' was the how-to-vote for candidates running jointly for the Australian Labor Party and the Communist Party of Australia. This was taken as proof of communist influence in the Labor Party. From this, the use of the term has broadened to cover any alliance between political groups that would not normally line up alongside each other or be thought of as suitable political partners. Thus the disapproving 1990s reference to a unity ticket between One Nation and the National Party.

## urger

A few are not poor; that flashily dressed young man is a professional gambler here to put on an off the course commission; that sharp-featured man with the darting eyes is an 'urger' who lives by attending the tote telling credulous people that he has a good tip—he persuades them to back a horse themselves and put a little on for him; as he gives a different tip to each person, he gets a few winners each day, and shows a profit.

Frank Hardy, *Power without Glory*, 1950.

To say that someone is 'a bit of an urger' means that you can't trust them. If they want you to do something, take care because they have their own interests at heart. This word hails from the racecourse where the 'urgers' or 'tipslingers', both terms which have been around since the early 1900s, worked for the bookmakers. Their job was to get as many people laying bets on as wide a range of horses as possible. The 'urger's' manner was friendly and confidential. He would convince the innocent punter that he had a hot tip and persuade the sucker to put his money on a horse that he, the 'urger', knew for a certainty was going to win. He would then move on to the next trusting gambler with a hot tip about a totally different horse. The scope of his activities then widened to any kind of minor scam in which the gullible were hoodwinked. And widened again from small but specific con jobs to any kind of activity in which the 'urger' was taking advantage of others.

# (Vv)

## vegemite

Perhaps it was being back in Melbourne that put him out of sorts, or maybe he was practising his snarly Dame Edna character. Whatever it was, rotund funnyman Barry Humphries was not at all a happy little Vegemite when he visited one of Melbourne's 'in' restaurants, Orexis, in Brunswick St, Fitzroy, on Logies' eve.

*Herald* (Melbourne), 1990.

This thick, black, salty yeast extract, a by-product of beer-making, has been part of the Australian food scene since it was developed in 1922 by Cyril Callister. It is mostly used as a spread on sandwiches and toast, though there is such a thing as 'vegemite broth', made by spooning some vegemite straight from the jar into some boiled water.

In 1928 vegemite was relaunched as 'Parwill', that is, 'Pa will', as opposed to Marmite, 'Ma might', a feeble pun which produced little result in sales. The original name was re-adopted and promoted vigorously—the advertising jingle which rang out across the nation's airwaves, and later, television channels, 'We're happy little vegemites, As bright as bright can be', has spawned the colloquial expression 'happy little vegemite' to refer to someone who is extremely pleased. This is often used ironically. If your partner gets up out of the wrong side of the bed, slips in the bathroom, spills milk all over the paper, and then sits at the kitchen table glowering, you cannot help but say, 'Who's a happy little vegemite, then?'

## veranda

The house comprised three rooms in a row, light and cheap in construction, but comfortable, with a raised wooden floor, papered walls, a fireplace, a slabbed veranda with a garden strip in front of it, and a grass plot adjoining for bleaching clothes.

Frank Dalby Davison, *The Road to Yesterday*, 1964.

This shady extension to a building is an architectural feature that we picked up from India where the word is found in languages like Hindi and Bengali. The concept (and the word) was borrowed there from Portuguese and Spanish culture, the word 'varanda' in those languages meaning a 'railing' or 'balustrade', which just goes to show how a good idea can travel the world. The spelling 'verandah' is an attempt to capture the long final 'a' of the borrowed word.

The Australian terrace house 'veranda' does seem to be of our own making, as are some of the iron lace patterns created in local foundries from about 1850. We talk about this decorative feature as 'wrought iron' though the panels are commonly cast rather than wrought. Wrought iron was of course highly original, expensive and upmarket as opposed to the mass-produced cast-iron panels.

The figure on the veranda who directs operations while others do the work is the 'veranda manager' or the 'veranda boss'. 'Veranda pearlers' are people who own the pearling luggers (and collect the profits) but never venture out to sea. With this exception in contemporary English 'veranda' seems to have been replaced by 'armchair' in making similar compounds, such as 'armchair critic'.

# (Ww)

## walkabout

> 'But where's your pack and where have you been? Why
> did you go walkabout?'
> 'I thought you might be getting tired of me.'
> 'Well maybe, but just to vanish! We were concerned.'
> Neilma Sidney, 'A Stranger in the Dordogne' in
> *Sunday Evening*, 1988.

A 'walkabout' in colonial times was another name for a
swagman or itinerant, a word deriving from Aboriginal pidgin.
So when the white settlers described the Aborigines as 'going
walkabout' they were invoking the same notion of shiftless-
ness and untrustworthiness that they attached to the swaggies.
The settlers had no notion of the patterns of life or passing of
ceremonies that dictated the presence or absence of the
Aborigines.

In mainstream Australian English the phrase 'go walka-bout' was used in connection with some item that was missing or lost, or a person who had suddenly disappeared. It was also a colloquial, slightly jocular expression for going on holiday. A greater understanding of Aboriginal culture, however, has led to the feeling that such use is patronising so the expression is disappearing.

## wallaby track

There are others who stick during shearing,
Then shoulder their swags on their back;
For the rest of the year they'll be steering
On their well-beloved Wallaby Track.
E. J. Overbury, 'The Wallaby Track' in *Bush Poems*,
1865.

---

The distinction we draw between 'kangaroo' and 'wallaby', that the former is large and the latter is small, is similar to the one that the Aborigines made. These words are drawn from two different Aboriginal languages. 'Kangaroo' was recorded by Captain Cook in his dealings with the Aborigines near the Endeavour River in Queensland. 'Wallaby' comes from the Port Jackson Aborigines, where it contrasted with their word for the larger kangaroo—'wallaroo'.

In Australian English, 'wallaby' has developed a wider range of meanings. People noticed the tracks made by wallabies in long grass. The tendency of two-legged wanderers to follow ready-made tracks led to the expression 'on the wallaby track', then reduced to 'on the wallaby'. The earliest example of the use of this phrase is dated 1849 and it is clear, from this and other examples, that the term described the well-worn paths from one bush dwelling to another followed by swagmen and itinerant bush workers in the hope of a job or some tucker. These travellers were then referred to as 'wallaby trackers'.

## waltzing Matilda

> Leaving Buninyong the doctor met a group of disappointed diggers, who were waltzing Matilda back to Melbourne, on the chance of finding fresh fields.
>
> Frank Clune, *Dig: A Drama of Central Australia*, 1937.

Banjo Paterson was an excellent folklorist and balladist with an ear for the vernacular. Such people sometimes freeze in a poem a word or phrase which had some currency in their day but which has since become obsolete. This seems to be the case with 'waltzing Matilda'.

The best suggestion as to its origin is that the phrase comes to us from the German community in South Australia. 'Mathilde' was a common name for a girlfriend—like 'Sheila' in Ireland. It was also a name for a coat, blanket or bed-roll, these being a substitute source of warmth and comfort when a flesh and blood 'Mathilde' was not available.

'Walzen' meant to go round and round as in the dance, but it also described other apparently aimless or circular travels. An apprentice setting out on a journey from town to town to further his knowledge of his craft was said to go 'waltzing'. A 'Walzbruder' or 'rolling brother' was a tramp.

The phrase, 'waltzing Matilda', was, however, an Australian coinage and in all probability came via the melting pot of the goldfields. At the end of the 1800s the phrase had variants such as 'walking Mathilde', 'humping Mathilde', 'letting Mathilde down at the door', but the popularity of Paterson's ballad has made 'waltzing' the recognised form.

There is a lesser-known explanation, that 'Matilda' was the name of the first woman swaggie who was Queen of the Road in Victoria. In truth, the likelihood of 'Matilda the Swaggie' existing at all is extremely remote.

## warrigal

The skinning of the black dingo was finished, and Tug, his pipe alight, was well on the way to the camp. He was stumping along in high spirits, living over again the moment when his finger had closed on the trigger. Neither then, nor during the long wait in the shadow of the brigalow, had any sense of fellowship with the

> warrigal stirred in his mind. It was hunter and hunted,
> and when his shot rang out the hunter had triumphed.
> Frank Dalby Davison, 'Return of the Hunter' in
> *The Wells of Beersheba*, 1933.

The dingo was the domesticated dog of the Aborigines—the same dog in the wild they called a 'warrigal'. Both words are from the Sydney language and documented in the early days of our colonial history.

Both words developed a range of meanings in Australian English. The essential quality of a warrigal was seen by the Europeans to be its untamed nature. White settlers divided the Aborigines into two groups—those who became part of white society and culture, and those who lived outside it—the warrigals. Horses also were divided into the tamed and the untamed, so that 'warrigal', at least until the 1930s, was another word for a brumby.

**wattle**

> Very many species of *acacia* are found in Australia…
> Locally, they are know by the name of wattles, from the
> slender twigs being used for that purpose.
> R. Mudie, *The Picture of Australia*, 1829.

'Wattle' is a name that has come from describing what the plant is good for rather than what the plant is. We have the name 'acacia', but the name 'wattle' comes from British dialect where a 'wattle' is a twig. The 'wattles' placed on a roof to support the thatch were often from trees like the willow that yielded supple twigs, easily bent and woven into a framework. 'Wattle and daub cottages' are structures which rely on a 'wattle' support for clay or mud filling. When the European settlers built their houses in colonial times they looked for 'wattle' and found that the acacia bushes did just as good a job as the willow back in England. Part of the charm of the 'wattle' is that it combines romanticism—the golden clusters of flowers—with functionalism—its usefulness to the colonists.

Don't be tricked—the 'wattlebird' did not get its name because it fancies the 'wattle tree' but because of 'the wattles'—fleshy lobes hanging from its neck—which are its distinguishing feature.

## whinge

Motty had a bad cold, and went whooping about the house, whingeing between whoops and clinging to Mumma's leg like a limpet.

Ruth Park, *Poor Man's Orange*, 1949.

We need to look at the history of 'whinge' in British English. The word 'whine' was an attempt to capture the sound of an arrow whizzing past. The sound that dogs make when they are unhappy seemed not unlike the sound of the arrow, so 'whine' extended its meaning. Finally a British northern dialect produced a variant of this—'whinge'.

Australians have done much more with this word than the British ever did. For us it has become a key item in our cultural lexicon. We teach our children not to 'whinge', we applaud ourselves as 'non-whingers', and we turn the tables on the British and label them the 'whingeing Poms' when they seem to spend an inordinate amount of time criticising Australia.

## wigwam for a goose's bridle

No one could explain the two copper objects Rob had found in the wash-house, but everyone was agreed that there was only one thing they could be. They were false teeth for a horse. He was satisfied with that. Sometimes when he asked what something was they would say: 'It's a triantiwontigong. It's a wigwam for a goose's bridle.' That made him furious.

Randolph Stow, *The Merry-Go-Round in the Sea*, 1965.

The phrase 'a wigwam for a goose's bridle' is used when you are asked to identify something and you either can't or don't want to answer. In this way it can be the equivalent of a 'watchamacallit' or a 'dooverlackie'. Although this odd saying is from British dialect, its usage on this continent is steeped in Australian history. The story goes that the bushranger Ben Hall used it when he held up a hotel in Tarago, near Goulburn, New South Wales. After demanding food and drink, Hall kindly offered to mind the baby while the lady of the establishment prepared his meal. Upon the arrival of the food, he exclaimed, 'Fair exchange! A wing-wong for a goose's bridle.'

In British dialect a 'whim-wham' was a trinket or knick-knack that could be put on a horse's bridle, but not a goose's. That was the original whimsicality of the expression. It was only later that 'whim-wham' was changed to 'wigwam' as a familiar if, in context, meaningless word. The substitution of course makes the phrase hopelessly opaque.

## willy-willy

> A willy-willy travels across the plain; the wind spins a bundle of weeds high into the air and heads up the valley. It comes to the trees, lingers for a while and then, skirting the grove, hurries toward the horizon.
>
> B. Wongar, *Walg*, 1983.

The 'willy-willy' is a whirlwind that can vary in size from a small flurry of leaves to a powerful column over ten metres in height. This is an Aboriginal borrowing—the doubling is a strong indication—but it could be either from Yindjibarndi, the language spoken in the Hamersley Range of Western

Australia, or from Wembawemba, the language spoken in western Victoria. I remember a Nyungar elder from Western Australia telling the story of the spirit in the 'willy-willy', of how it had threatened to overcome him but he put out his hand and touched the spirit and it went away. There is some evidence that 'willy-willy' is used figuratively in the same way as whirlwind, although there is a touch of self-consciousness about this usage.

## witchetty grub

> The chances were she had already served up to an unsuspecting Harold portions of disguised python, witchetty grub and bungarra, pandanus-nut, baked snake, stewed flying-fox, and scones from zamia-palm flour.
>
> Coralie and Leslie Rees, *Spinifex Walkabout*, 1953.

By meaning extension the name of the implement used to snare this grub became the name of the grub itself. 'Witchetty' is probably borrowed from the Adnyamathanha language of the Flinders Ranges in South Australia. The word breaks down into 'wityu' meaning 'hooked stick used to extract grubs' and 'varti' meaning 'grub'. Literally, 'witchetty' is a 'grub hook', and indeed the earliest citation from 1862 has the word with exactly this meaning. This transfer of meaning from the implement to the grub itself is evident in the 1890s. The grub is the larva of any of a number of moths and beetles which can be eaten raw or cooked, and is said to have the flavour of almonds.

## wog

Isn't it just tipical of my luck that I get a Scarlet Fever wog in the long Vac when earlier it could have saved me six weeks of that miner hell they call school.

Dymphna Cusack, *Black Lightning*, 1964.

It is surprising that the origin of this word is a mystery but no dialect dictionary has anything resembling it. It made its appearance in print in the early 1900s which means it probably had a nineteenth-century existence in the spoken language, particularly since it is such a domestic and informal word, especially common among children.

Initially, it referred to grubs, insects, beetles and creepy-crawlies of any description. Sidney J. Baker wrote that in the 1940s the meaning had extended to cover microbes or germs, thought of as internal creepy-crawlies. A 'wog' is any such microbe that makes you ill, but 'the wog' is commonly a synonym for the flu since that is usually the illness that is going around, while a specified 'wog', such as the scarlet fever wog in the quotation above, describes a particular complaint.

This meaning of 'wog' is not to be confused with the British and Australian colloquial term for someone from the Mediterranean or Middle East, often explained as an acronym for 'westernised' or 'wily oriental gentleman' but more reasonably explained as short for 'golliwog'. This was a derogatory term which has been turned into a badge of pride, at least in Australia.

## wombat

> At the third point a huge log, heavy enough to tax the thews of a strong man, had been bodily unearthed and contemptuously tossed aside...He then suggested a more deeply sunken barricade at the various points of entry. As he explained, wombats, in one aspect, resemble a certain type of politician; they are dogged possessors of single-track minds.
>
> C. J. Dennis, 'Warmbats: The Gardener's Foe', c. 1930.

Like many Aboriginal borrowings, 'wombat' started out in English with a variety of spellings. In colonial times we experimented with 'wambat', 'whombat', 'whombatt', 'womat', 'wombach' and 'womback'. One theory is that the large number of different spellings reflects dialectal differences within the Dharug language from which it was borrowed. In the early 1900s 'wombat' was used to mean 'a stupid person'.

Indeed, this characteristic dominates the personality of the 'Muddle-headed Wombat', but as a term of abuse it seems limited by the great affection which we all seem to have for this animal.

## wongi

'Oh well, let's get goin'. I want to have a bit of a wongi with you. Come on back to the homestead.'
Xavier Herbert, *Capricornia*, 1938.

In 1984 Senator Reg Withers startled the Canberra journos by revealing that he was known as the 'wongi man'. The first irreverent question asked was whether that was Aboriginal for 'toecutter', that being his other nickname. The senator went on to say that 'wongi' was from the Nyungar language of Perth and meant 'to sit down and talk'. This was the senator's Dr Jekyll to the toecutter Mr Hyde. It is also a good example of how a word can gain currency if it is propelled into the limelight by a politician or 'media personality'. In this case the limelight flickered briefly and 'wongi', while known in the west, would still be a blank to most people in the east. It is a word that can be found in a number of Aboriginal languages of the west and the central desert, and, as a verb, means 'to speak or talk' and, as a noun, means 'language'.

## wood-and-water joey

It's all devilish fine for you and your brother and the Captain there to go flashin' about the country and sporting your figure on horseback, while I'm left alone to do the housekeepin' in the Hollow. I'm not going to be wood-and-water Joey, I can tell ye, not for you nor no other men...

Rolf Boldrewood, *Robbery under Arms*, 1889.

Wood and water were the essential commodities that had to be supplied to the camp and that involved tedious and unskilled labour. The 'joey' element goes back to goldmining days when the goldfields population was roughly divided up into the miners, the police and the hangers-on. The Governor of Victoria at the time was Charles Joseph La Trobe who was unpopular with the miners, and so the troopers, as La Trobe's representatives, were referred to as 'Joes'. From there it became a general term of derision.

## Woop-Woop

'Listen, Mr Wilkerson,' I says, 'I'm awake-up, I am. Ya doan need ter come that stuff with me. I didden come down in the last shower. Where d'ya think I come from? Woop Woop?'

Lawson Glassop, *We Were the Rats*, 1944.

'Woop-Woop' is meant to sound Aboriginal with its typical reduplication. The records show that by the early 1900s it was established as a mythical outback town. Less successful was the attempt to create a stereotypical inhabitant of such a town, called a 'woop'. We can make no sense from this distance of the actual choice of sounds but can only guess that they originally sounded comical. Similarly, Bullamakanka may just have been an amusing invention, although there is the suggestion that it comes from Aboriginal pidgin *bulla macow* meaning 'bully beef', More complicated still is Oodnagalahbi, which breaks down into a shortened form of Oodnadatta combined with 'galah' and the suffix '-bi' as a pretend Aboriginal marker of place.

In contrast to these fictitious places we have 'Hay, Hell and Booligal', where Hay and Booligal are real enough and Hell is placed in between to convey how hot and unpleasant they all are. While the invented three placenames conjure up remoteness and lack of sophistication, Hay, Hell and Booligal are the ultimate in discomfort.

## wowser

Joggins was a living personification of the term 'wowser'. He was a little man with a thin ascetic face, and a gleam of wild fanaticism in his eyes. To him the seven deadly sins were gambling, drinking alcoholic liquor, horse-racing, telling smutty stories, hotel-keeping, fornication and young people of opposite sexes consorting together.

Frank Hardy, *Power without Glory*, 1950.

---

A 'wowser' is someone puritanical in the extreme, someone who is implacable in their opposition to sinfulness. This word comes from the British dialect word 'wow' meaning to howl as a dog does. It is the second element of the familiar 'bow-wow', the standard representation of a dog's bark. At first a 'wowser' was someone who made a lot of noise either in complaint or just general uproarious behaviour. In 1879 a wowser was someone who was 'beastly drunk'. The term was then applied to political discontents and wild women. But even while that meaning was still in use, another developed, the one we know today of the censorious person. This use of 'wowser' was given a boost by John Norton, editor of the *Truth* newspaper in the 1890s, who, for his own purposes, reinvented its etymology as an acronym for the slogan 'We Only Want Social Evils Remedied'.

# (Yy)

## yabby

> Yabbies: Fresh water crustaceans lured from muddy dams with lumps of rancid meat tethered to pieces of string. A delicacy second only to the Choo-Choo Bar.
>
> Phillip Adams, *The Unspeakable Adams*, 1974.

The 'yabby' is the freshwater crayfish native to south-eastern Australia. In Queensland they are known as 'lobbies'— 'lobster' cut short with an '-ie' ending. The form 'yabby' had earlier variations like 'yabber' which attempted to capture the Wembawemba word 'yabij'. The Wembawemba language from which the word was taken was spoken in north-western Victoria. Unfortunately, we don't know why the word borrowed from this area became accepted up and down the eastern part of Australia. In Western Australia the local, much-larger crayfish was referred to as the 'marron', a borrowing from the Nyungar language spoken near Perth. The marine equivalent of this delicacy is the 'shovel-nosed lobster' known as the 'Balmain bug' or the 'Moreton Bay bug' depending on your regional perspective.

## yakka

For those who wish to pursue a veterinary career Anne considers a rapport with animals essential. 'You have to like animals and you have to enjoy working with them. It's not all glamor, there's a lot of hard yakka involved.'
*Sunday Sun* (Melbourne), 1989.

'Hard yakka' is the ultimate Aussie phrase for a stint of good solid work. Yet however much we relish the phrase, we still seem undecided about the spelling which varies from 'yakka' to 'yacca' to 'yacka'. The expression remains a colloquialism—part of the spoken rather than the written language, a bush word and a rural word, so this might account for the absence of a standard form. It first appears in the late 1800s in Brisbane where it was borrowed from the Yagara language, but by the early 1900s it had travelled to the west appearing in the *Jarraland Jingles* of 1908. City slickers adopt it in a half-joking fashion.

## yeo

> Out on the board the old shearer stands,
> Grasping his shears in his thin bony hand,
> Fixed is his gaze on a bare-bellied yeo—
> Glory if he gets her won't he make the ringer go.
> > Anon, 'Click Go the Shears', c. 1800s.

'Click Go the Shears' has a number of interesting items for the student of Australian English. First, there is 'yeo', a minor British dialect form of the standard 'ewe'. In some versions, 'yeo' has become 'joe' in an effort to make the words familiar, if not exactly sensible. The yeo is 'bare-bellied' because it has defective wool growth which causes the wool to drop off its legs and belly.

Various colonial stereotypes are identified in the verses of this famous song. First there is the 'colonial-experiencer', that is, the man sent out from Britain to experience life in the colonies, either because his ultimate job back home was going to be in industries like wool, or because it was a character-building exercise, fostering such qualities as self-reliance and adaptability. The writer of this ballad is full of sarcasm for this blow-in from the city ('just got off his horse' and yet he acts as if he knows everything).

The 'new chum' is there, as is 'the boss of the board', that is, the man in charge of the shearing (the 'board' being that section of the shearing shed where the sheep are shorn). And if the new chum manages to get all the sheep out of the paddock, then he may yet make a 'jackeroo', which is at least one step up the ladder in the hierarchy of station life.

## youse

'You know this is just like Alec,' Bunny Benfield said, stopping to mop his brow. 'I remember him saying: "Youse buggers are going to be sorry one of these days that you didn't do a good job clearing that cemetery while you was at it." If he's anywhere about, I bet he's laughing his head off...'
    Kylie Tennant, *Lost Haven*, 1946.

This despised pronoun is a hand-me-down from Irish English into both Australian and American English. The *English Dialect Dictionary* lists it as the dialectal plural form of 'you'. It's a pity really that it didn't ever become part of the standard dialect in Australia and America, because it would be handy to be able to tell whether one person or more than one person is meant. Imagine you are in a crowded room and say 'Are you coming?' Are you addressing one person or all of them?

Perhaps the Irish origin of the word made it less prestigious in Australian English, the Irish being mostly political prisoners and regarded as troublemakers in colonial Australia. By the time all that was behind us, 'youse' was regarded as such a no-no that I doubt that it can ever achieve respectability. A matter of regret? 'What do youse think?' And, as you can tell, I mean all of you.

## yowie

Thanks to a buffer of doubt, a murky no-man's land between them, they were able to continue, as a reflex almost, putting favours each other's way, as one might put out a saucer of milk for a prowling yowie, that wild creature never yet seen by white man but known for its periodic forays into tearing the heads off bulls…observed emerging from the night, unsuspecting but cautious all the same, docile enough to make straight for the milk but savage when cornered, and against whom no net in the world could be guaranteed secure…

Rodney Hall, *Kisses of the Enemy*, 1987.

The shaggy man-like creature of the wild seems to be one that lurks in the human imagination. There is the 'abominable snowman', the 'alma', the 'big-foot', the 'sasquatch' and the 'yeti'. To that list the Aborigines have added the 'douligah' and the 'yowie'. In the mysterious way in which language works, the 'yowie' has become well-known though not quite as popular as the 'bunyip'.

The word 'yowie' came from the Yulwaalaraay language spoken by the Aborigines near Lightning Ridge in outback New South Wales. The 'douligah' is from speakers of the Dhurga and Dharawal languages living around Jervis Bay, New South Wales. Who can say why the 'yowie' prospered, even being elevated to fame as a chocolate, while the 'douligah' still lurks in the linguistic shadows.

THE EXPLORERS
**edited and introduced by Tim Flannery**

'Tim Flannery is in the league of the all-time explorers
like Dr David Livingstone.'
Sir David Attenborough

'Traces the face and searches for the heart of this extraordinarily varied continent which we do not properly know…it is humbling to find these stories new and relevant…read *The Explorers*, to help with your own exploration of Australia, and therefore of yourselves.'
Bary Dowling, *Sydney Morning Herald*

'Tim Flannery takes a part of Australian history that has meant numbing boredom to generations of schoolchildren, and pummels it into robust and tragicomic shape.'
*Bulletin*

'Exploration is an important part of Australian history and *The Explorers* serves as an introduction into that wave which over a few hundred years may be seen as one of the prime motivations or factors behind the formation of a modern Australian identity.'
*Courier-Mail*

'Tim Flannery's utterly compelling anthology, documenting almost four centuries of exploration, takes us beyond the frontier into a world of danger, compassion, humour, brutality and death… Here in one place, is the most remarkable body of non-fiction writing ever produced in Australia.'
*Geelong Advertiser*

400pp, paperback, rrp$23.00, ISBN 1 876485 22 1

# THE LIFE & ADVENTURES OF WILLIAM BUCKLEY
## by JOHN MORGAN
### edited and introduced by Tim Flannery

On Sunday, 6 July 1835, an enormous man shambled into the camp left by John Batman near Geelong. Though clearly a European, he spoke no English. He bore a tattoo on his arm, of the letters WB alongside rough drawings of the sun, moon and what appeared to be a possum. To the amazement of those in the camp, when he was given a slice from a loaf, he suddenly uttered the word 'bread'.

'Buckley was also well and truly aware of how to spin a yarn. Keep your wits about you as you read, cautions Flannery. It's unique history.'
*Courier-Mail*

'This account, in Buckley's words…has all the elements of a *Boy's Own* yarn: convicts, savages, privations, wars, cannibalism, survival, treachery and the founding of a colony…remarkable.'
*Herald Sun*

'Dr Flannery has done us a service first by reissuing the story of a fascinating adventure from 200 years ago, and then by setting these events in perspective with his lucid introduction…a great read!'
*Canberra Times*

248pp, paperback, rrp$23.00, ISBN 1 877008 20 6

TERRA AUSTRALIS
Matthew Flinders' Great Adventures in the
Circumnavigation of Australia
**edited and introduced by Tim Flannery**

First published in 1814, in two volumes, this is the enthralling
account of the circumnavigation of Australia, by the man who
gave our country its name.

'With a series of finely edited versions of Australian historical
classics, of which *Terra Australis: Matthew Flinders' Great
Adventures in the Circumnavigation of Australia* is the latest
instalment, Tim Flannery and Text Publishing have made
Australian history interesting again.'
*Australian's Review of Books*

'A superb evocation of Australia. A fascinating document.'
*Sun-Herald.*

'Flinders' detailed stories remain vivid to this day…described
with the backdrop of the unforgettable wilderness of Australia.'
*Lobbyist*

'Tim Flannery's efforts in editing Matthew Flinders' Journals
of his circumnavigation of Australia make them far more
interesting than the original.'
*Asia Pacific Shipping*

312pp, paperback, rrp$22.00, ISBN 1 876485 92 2

# LION AND KANGAROO
## The Initiation of Australia
### Gavin Souter

'Souter is a writer of great distinction…This book is the work
of a man who can impose on the chaos of the past an order that
lifts the work into the realms of art without doing violence to
the events or sacrificing the standards of scholarship as defined
by the academics. It is a great achievement.'
Manning Clark

'A superb evocation of Australian life in the years between
federation and the First World War, showing how imperial
sentiment dominated our lives and left a vacuum in Australia's
national identity…Souter's book is beautifully written, lucid,
witty and compelling.'
Gough Whitlam

'A masterpiece…The book, assiduously researched for its
making, is materially explosive, especially the chapters
"Gallipoli", "Pozières" and "The War in Australia"…Souter
lets the material do its own erupting, then shapes it to his
magnificent control…A mighty work of history.'
*Courier-Mail*

'The best Australian book to have come my way in a long
time…It is mature, balanced, witty and entertaining, and it is
beautifully written…It combines the care of the historian with
the journalist's flair for the picturesque and eye for character.'
*Australian*

448pp, paperback, rrp$22.00, ISBN 1 876485 75 2

# THE MAN WHO LOST HIMSELF
## The Unbelievable Story of the Tichborne Claimant
**Robyn Annear**

In 1854, the *Bella* foundered off the coast of South America. On board was Roger Tichborne, heir to a baronetcy and estates in England. No survivors were found and Roger was presumed dead—except by his mother. Twelve years later, a bankrupt Australian butcher named Tom Castro claimed to be the missing heir. This rollicking, convoluted true story is retold with energy and wit by Robyn Annear. *The Man Who Lost Himself* is a story of thwarted love, sexual ambiguity, class and family warfare and courtroom drama.

'A compelling read.'
*Sydney Morning Herald*

'More twists and turns than a funfair hall of mirrors'
*Herald Sun*

'A popular history that resembles a work of fiction, not only in its fabulous plot twists but in its wry, engaging narrative style, witty re-creation of dialogue, and vivid animation of characters and scenery…this book, like any good whodunit, rewards rereading.'
*Age*

'An engrossing story, told with the wit and verve of a comic novelist.'
*Bulletin*

448pp, paperback, rrp$32.00, ISBN 1 877008 17 6